CHALLENGES FOR THE SINGAPORE ECONOMY AFTER THE GLOBAL FINANCIAL CRISIS

CHALLENGES FOR THE SINGAPORE ECONOMY AFTER THE GLOBAL FINANCIAL CRISIS

Editor

Peter Wilson
School of Economics,
Singapore Management University

 **World Scientific**

NEW JERSEY · LONDON · SINGAPORE · BEIJING · SHANGHAI · HONG KONG · TAIPEI · CHENNAI

Published by

World Scientific Publishing Co. Pte. Ltd.

5 Toh Tuck Link, Singapore 596224

USA office: 27 Warren Street, Suite 401-402, Hackensack, NJ 07601

UK office: 57 Shelton Street, Covent Garden, London WC2H 9HE

British Library Cataloguing-in-Publication Data
A catalogue record for this book is available from the British Library.

CHALLENGES FOR THE SINGAPORE ECONOMY AFTER THE
GLOBAL FINANCIAL CRISIS

ISBN-13 978-981-4343-93-0
ISBN-10 981-4343-93-5

Typeset by Stallion Press
Email: enquiries@stallionpress.com

Printed in Singapore.

PREFACE

It has been claimed that the 2008–2009 global financial crisis produced the most serious recession since the Great Depression in the 1930s. Thanks to the united efforts of governments and central banks worldwide, we have had the good fortune of avoiding a full-blown global depression. Nonetheless, the global economy after the crisis is clearly different from before.

Given the scale of the crisis, important questions must be and have been asked. Primary among them are Why? and How? Knowing why the crisis developed allows us to avoid the same mistakes that caused the crisis in the first place. Understanding the mechanisms behind how the crisis unfolded and escalated enables us to correct the areas that exacerbated the problems.

Just as important, however, is the question of 'What now?'. Questions of 'Why?' and 'How?' are backward-looking. 'What now?' is forward-looking. It is a question concerned with the future. It is a question targeted at policy-makers and is a question that is very often asked in Singapore, where there is a clear recognition that sound economic policy serves as the bedrock for sustained future economic growth.

This book attempts to shed light on this question. A well-thought plan must involve consideration of various challenges and obstacles that may be faced. This is where this book comes in. It brings together some of the best minds in their respective fields to discuss the challenges that post-crisis Singapore faces and consequently, the best path forward. The nature of the book is highly topical with a consistent underlying focus on Singapore and the challenges faced. The topics vary widely. That is to be expected since the challenges are myriad, ranging from growth issues to equity issues and spanning both domestic and international arenas.

Every challenge presents an opportunity. The same is true for Singapore in the post-crisis era. The 2008–2009 crisis was vicious in causing retrenchment and unemployment. However, it also provided time and opportunities for economic transformation at the country level towards environmentally sustainable development. During the financial crisis, lower global demand meant that commercial activity and business transactions were slower in most industries, lowering the cost of raw materials. The lower opportunity accounting cost provided incentives for industries to incorporate energy efficiency considerations into the design of their industrial facilities as well as to adopt energy efficient technologies with some financial support and subsidies from the government. Apart from the positive environmental effect, these upfront investments should also improve production efficiency and lower business cost in the long run, preparing firms for the good times ahead by keeping them competitive in the global business arena.

The above serves as an illustration of one of the opportunities that arise from the challenge of the global financial crisis. Others will be taken apart, analysed, and synthesised in subsequent chapters by experts in various areas of economics. It is my hope that this book will serve to illuminate the key issues that Singapore faces in the uncertain post-crisis era and provide sound information for pragmatic policy design. On that note, I wish all readers an enjoyable and constructive journey through the pages that follow.

Euston Quah
Professor of Environmental Economics
Nanyang Technological University, Singapore
Editor, *Singapore Economic Review*

CONTENTS

INTRODUCTION

Peter Wilson

"Here all is life and activity; it would be difficult to name a place on the face of the globe with brighter prospects or more pleasant satisfaction. In little more than three years, it has risen from an insignificant fishing village to a large and prosperous town, containing at least ten thousand inhabitants...."

(Stanford Raffles)[1]

With hindsight Singapore escaped relatively unscathed from the 2008–2009 global crisis as far as the direct financial fallout is concerned apart from a fall in equity prices and some losses by Singapore's *de facto* sovereign wealth funds. The impact of the crisis on the 'real' economy was, however, much more dramatic as the slowdown in weighted GDP growth in Singapore's major trading partners (apart from India and China) in 2009 was transmitted to Asia and Singapore through the trade channel. As it transpired, the real rebound in Singapore was not to come until the second and third

---

[1] Cited in Nigel Barley (2010: 268).

quarters of 2009 following four consecutive quarters of sequential contraction in GDP.

However, the widely expected severe and prolonged contraction did not materialize such that by April 2010 Singapore had recovered all the output lost since the peak in the first quarter of 2008 and the official forecast for 2010 released in July was between 13% and 15%. Moreover, the impact on employment was much more muted than in previous downturns, undoubtedly helped by large nominal wage cuts, job creation in the construction and services sectors (integrated resorts) and budget stimulus initiatives in the 2009 and 2010 fiscal year budgets, including the Jobs Creation Scheme.

We begin in Chapter 2 with an overview of the impact of the global financial crisis on Singapore and post-crisis challenges ahead. This is followed by a summary of the main tenets of Singapore's economic policy strategy since independence in 1965 and some recent concerns and suggestions for a change in direction in some areas. The chapter is rounded off with the recommendations of the Government's 2010 Economic Strategies Committee, which addresses some of these issues.

Taking the long view, Manu Bhaskaran and Peter Wilson show that there has been a remarkable degree of continuity in Singapore's economic strategy since 1965, which has undoubtedly been helped by the fact that the government has been formed by the same party since 1959 and Singapore had one Prime Minister, Lee Kwan Yew from that time until 1990.

Policy-making in Singapore has always been heavily top-down with the government playing the role of entrepreneur in the sense of establishing organizations to support growth through Statutory Boards and a myriad of Government-Linked Companies (GLCs), many of which still survive today. In one way or another the government has a tight control over resources, including land. Savings are mobilized through the compulsory Central Provident Fund (CPF) and investment, especially in social and economic infrastructure, is targeted and directed through government or quasi-government organizations.

A key feature of Singapore's economic growth is that it has been overwhelmingly driven by exports, aided by large inflows of foreign capital and labour, and has been supported by policy commitments to free trade, regional integration and export promotion. As a consequence, growth cycles in Singapore are strongly affected by swings in external demand. This, together with a heavy dependence on foreign labour and multinational corporations (MNCs), has tended to be viewed as an inevitable consequence of Singapore's dearth of natural and human resources and a necessary evil to achieving rapid growth in GDP and industrialization.

Macroeconomic policy has played an important complementary role by focusing on high savings through budget surpluses and the CPF and conservative fiscal and monetary policies have been aimed at maintaining long-run competitiveness by keeping consumer price inflation low and stable and attracting a steady stream of mobile foreign capital and labour. When necessary, especially during severe downturns, adjustment can be speeded up as a result of Singapore's flexible labour market, where a substantial portion of wages are now contingent on the performance of the economy and can be reduced to restore cost competitiveness. If that is not sufficient, then public-sector related cost-cuts can be implemented quickly.

Since Singapore competes largely without protection in the global economy, if there are periodic concerns about Singapore's long-run structural adjustment and ability to compete in a rapidly-changing world economy, then the traditional policy response has been 'diversification', both in terms of products produced and markets to sell to, 'restructuring' to increase value-added and 'upgrading' through a variety of government subsidized, but ultimately market related, training schemes.

There is no doubt that this strategy has been successful according to conventional indicators of economic development in transforming Singapore into a high income manufacturing and services economy with a substantial increase in welfare for the vast majority of its citizens. Moreover, rapid growth and industrialization have not been at the expense of macroeconomic stability. Price inflation has been low by international standards, there has been high employment most of the time, external government debt has been negligible, and there have been persistent surpluses on the balance of payments and a rapid accumulation of official foreign exchange reserves.

The post-crisis outlook for Singapore will pose many challenges, including increased volatility in external markets, the threat of slower global growth and rising protectionism and competitive challenges in financial services from Chinese cities, such as Shanghai, but there will also be opportunities as China and India continue to expand and Singapore benefits from being at the heart of an expanding Asian hinterland.

Although Singapore's economic strategy has been very successful since independence, there have been some concerns expressed by economists and others in the last decade or two that the Republic's growth and welfare performance may have fallen short of expectations and that the present underlying growth model may be unsustainable.

Real GDP growth appears to have slowed in the last decade and Singapore's growth cycle has become more volatile. The long-term 'catch-up' in productivity growth also appears to have stalled somewhat and looks especially weak in services industries, such as restaurants and real estate, and in construction. Some argue that Singapore might have become 'hooked' on cheap foreign labour to sustain growth which has adversely held down the wages of indigenous workers and acted as a disincentive to raise labour productivity. In particular, the issue of foreign workers, which now constitute about 35% of the total workforce, has become more controversial in recent decades.

At the same time, the domestic economy may have become too dependent on foreign-owned MNCs in the manufacturing sector, reinforced by the official determination to keep manufacturing at 20–25% of GDP. The negative side of rapid export-led growth may have been an excessive dependence on external demand and foreign resources and an increase in the volatility of the business cycle. Allied to this is the longer-term weakness that Singapore generally does very well in comparative studies of international business competitiveness but not so well in entrepreneurship and related activities, perhaps because of the extensive involvement of the government in the economy and the emphasis on manufacturing for export by large foreign companies.

Perhaps Singapore should reset the goal to 3–5% GDP growth and raise domestic labour productivity by reducing the number of foreign workers allowed into the Republic. There could also be a gradual shift in emphasis towards increasing domestic demand and the services sector and the role of decentralized market forces, together with greater help to small and medium-sized firms. This might move Singapore closer to its current competitive advantage as a knowledge-based hub and revitalize 'regionalization', on the assumption that Singapore has not done enough to take advantage of opportunities in the Asian region in its quest to diversify into global markets.

There have also been some doubts whether the 'trickle down' of the benefits of past growth has been sufficient to compensate for the sacrifices that Singaporean workers have made to keep the externally-oriented model working. One indicator of this has been rising income inequality as technological change benefits those with higher skills and knowledge and increases competition for jobs, reinforced by the meritocratic nature of Singaporean society and absence of comprehensive safety nets for the poor and unemployed and flaws in the design of the CPF system which has produced a number of retirees who are 'asset rich but cash poor'.

Some have called for a move away from a narrow focus on GDP as the barometer of success to criteria which are more explicitly 'inclusive' such as targets for income distribution or indicators of the quality of life. Others have suggested cuts in the CPF employee contribution rate or a rise in the employer's contribution, or even changes to the tax and benefit system to make it more redistributive, an issue which is very sensitive in Singapore.

The chapter finishes with a summary of the recommendations presented by the Economic Strategies Committee (ESC) set up by the government in May 2009 and whose findings were made public in February 2010.

The Committee accepted that in a cross-country comparison Singapore's productivity in manufacturing and services fell short of its peers and recommended institutional changes to help achieve a 2–3% target of productivity growth per year over the next decade.

They also recognized that some slowing in the inflow of foreign workers might be necessary through a rise in the Foreign Workers' Levy. Nonetheless, despite some laudable changes in policy, such as measures to improve energy efficiency and provide more help to smaller firms and those needing trade financing, the post-ESC strategy appears to be more of a continuation of the 'top-down, diversify and upgrade' model of the past with continued stress on export-led MNC-oriented growth and manufacturing remaining at 20% to 25% of GDP.

In Chapter 3, Basant Kapur offers some deep reflections on economic policy-making in Singapore and laments the narrow emphasis on 'growthmanship' or GDP growth as a measure of social welfare. He suggests that more time should be allowed for distributional issues, that public-sector bonuses should be linked to a broader measure of productivity growth and the well-being of lower paid Singaporeans than GDP per se and perhaps the tax system should be made more progressive to reduce income inequality.

This should be part of a more general change in emphasis in Singapore away from a local culture which puts great stress on material prosperity and examination-oriented performance criteria, towards one which would allow more space for 'passion' and comparative cultural studies in schools and more concern for others to enhance social cohesiveness. He cites the lack of access to subsidies for anti-retroviral drugs to combat HIV/AIDS as an example.

He is also in favour of increasing the role of domestic demand by increasing the ratio of consumer expenditure to GDP as in other small open economies, such as Hong Kong, perhaps by increasing the rate of release of land sales to moderate house price increases; and reconsidering the 'mixed blessing' of relying on unskilled foreign labour to propel growth, although increasing the Foreign Worker Levy should be done slowly to give firms time to adjust to the new environment.

Policy-making in Singapore does not operate in a vacuum but rather is significantly affected by external political events, including those in the Asian region. In Chapter 4, Pradumna R Rana carefully weighs up the reforms to the international financial architecture implemented after the Asian financial crisis of 1997–1998 and during the present global financial crisis and how they affect Singapore and Asia. In particular, he asks how Asia can further strengthen its participation in the Group of Twenty (G20) and other negotiating bodies.

Although some steps were taken after the Asian crisis to reform the governance of the International Monetary Fund and make it better equipped to deal with future crises, with some increases in quotas and voting rights in line with the greater importance of emerging economies, including those in Asia, progress so far has been slow. The broadening of the Group of Eight (G8) to the G20 and associated institutional changes to enhance peer review systems and reduce the likelihood of systemic failures are steps in the right direction, but it is still not clear what will be done with the 'left-out' countries.

His advice is to make sure that these 'left-out' countries are heard effectively at G20 meetings by making the present Association of South-East Asian Nations (ASEAN) representatives at G20 meetings more of a formal part of the proceedings, to arrange meetings of ASEAN+3 just prior to G20 meetings, to invite India, Australia and New Zealand to Asian regional negotiations once the new ASEAN+3 Macroeconomic Research Office (AMRO) is established in Singapore in May 2011 and to increase the dialogue between the ASEAN+3 and other developing countries.

The labour market has been a crucial ingredient in Singapore's economic strategy, both as a long-run source of growth and as a stabilizer during cyclical downturns. Chew Soon Beng and Rosalind Chew argue in Chapter 5 that Singapore has been successful in managing its labour market since independence because the government has adopted a 'strategic' rather than an 'adversarial' strategy of collective bargaining. There is no 'free lunch' in the form of universal unemployment benefits, as in Europe, and there is no state pension for the public sector. The emphasis instead was to set non-mandatory wage guidelines through the National Wages Council from 1972 onwards, try to increase productivity and wages by increasing the employers' CPF contribution rate after 1978 (which was not very successful), to make the system more flexible with monthly variable components after 1988 and, more recently, to adopt pro-market training schemes to keep Singaporean workers up to speed in the face of global competition. To ensure that 'no one is left out' schemes, such as Workfare are designed to provide basic help to low wage workers in concert with self-help bodies.

How have these policies changed as a result of the global crisis? Should they be further changed to enhance labour productivity?

They point out that in reaction to the 2008–2009 downturn the budgets for Fiscal Years 2009 and 2010 have provided temporary support for workers through the Jobs Creation Scheme and Skills Programme for Upgrading and Resilience (SPUR) and that some public sector jobs were created according to 'Keynesian' logic. The raising of the Foreign Workers' Levy in 2010 is the latest example of government initiatives to 'manage' the influx of foreign workers and raise labour productivity in the longer run. Their view is that wages should only be increased if there is productivity growth and inflation is kept low. Shorter business cycles and an increasingly competitive international environment may also require further fiscal support during a downturn.

Singapore has become increasingly enmeshed in a complex system of cross-border production networks in the Asian region since the early 1990s and China has emerged to become the epicentre of this fragmented universe as an assembler and exporter of final goods. Chapter 6 by Yunhua Liu reminds us of the increasing importance of China as a market for Singapore's goods and as a source of imports and how the relationship has changed within a few decades. In the early 1990s Singapore was still seen as competing with China in both exports to third markets and as a recipient of foreign direct investment. However, now that the Republic has moved up the value-added chain the relationship has become more complementary rather than competitive with China and Hong Kong together accounting for more than 20% of Singapore's exports. China is also Singapore's largest destination for foregin direct investment and Singapore's businessmen and officials have undoubtedly learnt some important lessons from their earlier collaborations with the Chinese authorities.

Tilak Abeysinghe, Himani and Jeremy Lim ask, in Chapter 7, whether Singapore should be concerned about the equity aspects of its healthcare financing system and if so how equity can be improved without unduly burdening taxpayers.

Singapore's mixture of public and private provision and low public expenditure cost (less than 4% of GDP) ensures that it scores high on many international comparative healthcare indicators but does poorly in terms of equity, largely due to higher 'out of pocket' expenditures by those hospitalized. Based on a data analysis of hospital expenditure of a large number of elderly citizens they conclude that there is no comprehensive cover after retirement when it is most needed. The majority of patients are in subsidized wards with insufficient savings and few have government or private insurance cover, so they are heavily reliant on family medical savings, which is a burden for low income families. Indeed, despite subsidies, the system is closely aligned to income levels and there may even be some regressiveness in the system.

They recommend that the government should take steps towards a more universal system of healthcare financing without abandoning the principle of individual responsibility. Maybe MediShield should be made compulsory and the age dependent premium structure be replaced with an income dependent premium structure in the form of a MediShield tax as a small fixed percentage of income. Making MediShield compulsory would provide some cross-subsidization from rich to poor, active to inactive and well to sick and would remove the incentive for adverse selection.

The next two chapters by Chow Hwee Kwan and Peter Wilson (Chapter 8) and Lee Soo Ann (Chapter 9) make a preliminary assessment of Singapore's monetary and fiscal policy responses to the recent global crisis and what lessons can be learned from it.

As far as monetary policy is concerned, while central banks in the developed world responded to the credit crunch in unorthodox ways, including the widespread use of 'quantitative easing', in Singapore as in other parts of Asia where the direct fallout from the crisis was less severe, monetary authorities tended to respond with more traditional policy tools by lowering interest rates or increasing money aggregates or widening the scope of liquidity offered to banks short of funds. However, given Singapore's rather unusual monetary policy, the 'traditional' monetary response was a little more complicated.

The priority in Singapore was to gain access to emergency US dollars reserves through a swap with the US Federal Reserve, prevent a mass withdrawal of bank deposits by guaranteeing them until 2010, ease the monetary policy stance and increase access to liquidity if needed by the local banks.

As overall domestic liquidity in Singapore trended downwards from the middle of 2008, despite a fall in interest rates in line with global rates, the response of Singapore's *de facto* central bank, the Monetary Authority of Singapore (MAS), was to 'loosen' the monetary policy stance by flattening the trade-weighted Singapore dollar (TWS$) policy band, the intermediate instrument of monetary policy, and then re-centring it downwards.

What are the implications of the crisis for monetary policy?

The financial impact of the crisis on Singapore was undoubtedly cushioned by the fact that the fall in non-bank loan growth, which occurred alongside the contraction in GDP, was less severe than in previous crises due to strong demand for credit in the building and construction industry and from the residential housing sector. Moreover, although monetary policy played a countercyclical role during the crisis, fiscal policy played an even larger role. Also important was the downward adjustment in nominal wages in the labour market to help reduce the real effective exchange rate. However, Chow and Wilson Conjecture as to whether MAS would, if necessary have resorted to extensive quantitative easing along the lines of the UK, US and Japan and conclude that there are no obvious constraints to them doing so if they believed it was absolutely necessary.

Singapore already had a number of safeguards in place to help weather the storm but in response to the crisis MAS has since tightened up supervision over off-balance sheet activities and the marketing of structured products and, as with many central banks, is considering on-going regulatory changes recommended by international bodies, such as the G20 and Basel Committee on Banking Supervision.

A key lesson from this crisis is whether central banks should tighten monetary policy pre-emptively in order to moderate asset price bubbles before they burst and threaten overall price stability and indeed the stability of the financial system itself. Chow and Wilson analyse the arguments for and against, and present some tentative evidence that monetary policy might be effective in leaning against upswings in property prices and stock prices in Singapore.

However, since it is extremely difficult to identify bubbles *ex ante* and using monetary policy to pre-empt bubbles building up makes monetary policy much more complicated to implement, it is unlikely the MAS would want to use monetary policy to address bubbles any time soon. Given the constraints under which the MAS currently operates, such as heavy exposure to external trade and financial shocks, and the use of a single monetary policy instrument (the TWS$) to achieve multiple macroeconomic goals, it seems more likely that macro-prudential measure will be used instead to address bubbles. Indeed, in response to the rise in local property prices in the third quarter of 2009 and in February 2010 the government released more land for development, disallowed borrowers from deferring property payments and raised stamp duty if a property is sold within one year of purchase.

Lee Soo Ann in Chapter 9 notes that the FY2010 budget is a departure from the government's previous emphasis on expenditure and revenue measures towards more supply-side initiatives to increase business efficiency and private investment.

After a careful examination of recent budgets he concludes that 'primary' deficits[2] are expected to recur in the future as healthcare and defence costs rise and special transfers to the poor (especially the retired poor) continue to increase while income taxes shrink with the ageing population and the imperative to keep income taxes low in Singapore to remain internationally competitive. On the other hand, substantially increasing the Goods and Services Tax (GST) might be politically difficult.

Nonetheless, according to his calculations, the government should be able to finance any budget deficit for a long time to come given its financial assets but this may require drawing further on past official foreign exchange reserves, especially if its portfolio investments abroad

---

[2] Operating revenue minus total expenditure.

are lower than in the past. Hence the shift in the 2009 and 2010 budgets away from including 'Net Investment Income' to 'Net Investment Returns' or expected long-term real returns on relevant assets.

The key challenge, it seems, is to increase investment and restructure the economy to raise long-term productivity growth but this will increase the fiscal burden and the need to draw down reserves. Savings will need to be reduced but this is made difficult by the low share of wages in GDP which, in turn, stems from the reliance on foreign labour and foreign investment. Multinationals may bring with them new technology but how far they can increase productivity depends on what they are doing in Singapore and how they respond to the tax benefits and infrastructure provided to them, which themselves increase the tax burden.

Partha Sen in Chapter 10 uses macroeconomic theory to try to understand Singapore's version of a managed floating exchange rate regime. Singapore has 'cocked a snook' at those who argue that exchange rate regimes have to be either freely floating or a hard peg, yet the 'basket, band and crawl' or 'BBC' regime adopted by the MAS since the early 1980s has been very successful.

Applying the 'S-S' model and the 'target zone' approach used elsewhere in the literature is difficult since there is no explicit information on the upper or lower bounds of the trade-weighted policy band used as a policy reference point by the MAS in the conduct of its monetary policy apart from informed guesses by academics and market participants. The MAS does not announce the band or commit to intervening to keep the TWS$ within that band all the time since it wants to avoid telling speculators exactly what it will do in any given circumstances to deter 'one-way bets' and it wants to retain the flexibility to intervene where necessary to pre-empt unusually volatile capital movements.

A more fruitful approach to understanding exchange rate policy in Singapore is to estimate a policy reaction function which encapsulates the special features of the Singapore regime, namely the exchange rate centred monetary policy adopted since 1981 in response to Singapore's exceptionally high level of openness to international trade and capital flows. For Singapore, the gap between actual and expected inflation is the key determinant of exchange rate policy together with the deviation of output from its trend value.

In the final chapter, Chapter 11, Chew Soon Beng and Rosalind Chew explore what they call Singapore's 'citizen-government partnership for social equity' since 1965, which seeks to provide for social equity through a mixture of self-reliance and government intervention, and how it has coped with the global crisis.

The core of the partnership is the 'individual responsibility approach' under which citizens must work and save for four basic goods: a home, healthcare for the family, insurance for the family, education for their children and a pension or annuity for old age. The partnership is predicated on the view that the provision of universal unemployment benefits and healthcare and pensions for public sector workers is unsustainable. Costs would rise unacceptably with the ageing of the population, fiscal deficits would put downward pressure on currencies and the purchasing power of savings, unemployment would fall in line with a deterioration in the general business climate, and the system would create a disincentive to work and an incentive to engage in 'free-riding'.

In Singapore, by contrast, lower spending on welfare means government budgets can be in surplus and can be used to subsidise education, healthcare and transport for the poor and market-based training schemes. Together with strong incentives to work this provides an environment in which Singapore can prosper by providing an accommodating business environment and full employment in a fast-moving and highly competitive international environment.

But this is not sufficient if there are periods of unemployment and the purchasing power of savings falls due to rises in the prices of housing and education or a depreciation of the currency. The role of government, therefore, is to provide job opportunities and preserve the purchasing power of savings, including those in the CPF and those locked up in the official foreign exchange reserves, with a supporting role from charitable organizations. This is particularly important during a downturn such as in 2008–2009. Despite its merits, the CPF has evolved into 'a scheme for many purposes' and a mixture of savings and investment. As a result some citizens have insufficient savings for their old age despite the minimum sum requirement. Increasing the minimum sum, and making the purchase of an annuity compulsory upon retirement starting from 2013, are recent attempts to overcome this problem.

According to Chew and Chew the government's response to the recent crisis is, in a sense, a continuation of the citizen-government partnership. The Jobs Credit Scheme and SPUR were introduced in 2009 to keep Singaporeans in employment during the crisis rather than lowering the employers' contribution to the worker's CPF fund, together with tax measures to help low income families and past reserves have been called on for the first time. The purchasing power of the Singapore dollar has not been compromised and, as in the past, the recovery has been fast with minimal unemployment in the interim period.

END NOTE

Barley, N (2010). *In the Footsteps of Stamford Raffles*. London: Monsoon Books.

Chapter

2

THE POST-CRISIS ERA: CHALLENGES FOR THE SINGAPORE ECONOMY

Manu Bhaskaran and Peter Wilson

"Economic development is something much wider and deeper than economics. Its roots lie outside the economic sphere, in education, organization, discipline and, beyond that, in political independence and a national consciousness of self-reliance."

> *Small is Beautiful — A Study of Economics As If People Mattered,*
> by E. F. Schumacher, 1973.

THE IMPACT OF THE GLOBAL CRISIS ON SINGAPORE

The primary trigger for the 2008–2009 global financial crisis was the crash in the US housing bubble, which had peaked at the beginning of 2006, and the subsequent spillover effects on the US sub-prime mortgage market, leading eventually to widespread financial failures and a global credit crunch as inter-bank lending

15

dried up.[3] Investment banks had strong incentives to maximize the sales of mortgage backed securities to increase the return on equity since they had been initially priced on the premise of rising house prices and rents. These banks thus had huge exposure to 'collateralized debt obligations' which were, in turn, insured with large insurance companies in the form of credit default swaps.

Financial institutions were beginning to write down the value of mortgage backed securities in their portfolios in 2007 but the first sign of a crisis came when the US investment bank Bear Stearns halted redemptions on two hedge funds linked to mortgages leading to a loss of confidence in securitized mortgages. One of the first victims was Northern Rock, a highly leveraged medium-sized mortgage lender in the UK which experienced a bank run in mid-September 2007. It had aggressively expanded its share of UK mortgage lending from 3.6% in 1999 to 9.7% in 2007 financed through the securitization of its assets. The Bank of England could not save it from bankruptcy and placed it in public ownership in early 2008. Then in September 2008, the US government took over mortgage providers Fannie Mae and Freddie Mac; US investment bank Lehman Brothers collapsed and the global insurance company AIG filed for bankruptcy.

As the credit crunch increased in September 2008, the effects were transmitted to the real sector as forecasts for growth in major industrial countries were revised down and heralded a decline in global GDP for the first time since World War II and a sharp contraction in world trade volumes. The National Bureau of Economic Research (NBER) officially dates the start of the US recession as December 2007 when nonfarm payroll employment fell, although real GDP growth gave mixed signals. House prices continued to fall in the first two quarters of 2008 driven by a fall in personal consumer expenditure and by the end of the year one sixth of homes had negative equity. The Dow Jones Industrial Average fell by over half between its peak of October 2007 and March 2009. The decline was broad-based but the automotive industry and financial sector were particularly badly affected.

---

[3] For the timeline of the crisis, see Asian Development Bank (2009a).

Initially, the effects on Europe appeared to be less profound but Euro-zone GDP and industrial output began to fall sharply in the second half of 2008 and Iceland's heavily-exposed banks collapsed in October. Japan had limited exposure to toxic assets but the economy had already begun to weaken in early 2008, driven by declines in exports and private investment.

As far as Singapore is concerned, in 2007 the economy grew by an impressive 8.2%, marking the fourth consecutive year of strong growth (Table 1). The seasonally-adjusted headline unemployment rate was at a decade low of 1.6% in December of that year and 2.1% for the year as a whole or 3.0% for the resident population (Table 2). Even in the first quarter of 2008 GDP growth continued to be firm at 7.3% year on year (Y-O-Y) and 17.2% on a sequential basis and was broad-based across all sectors of the economy (Table 1 and Table 3)

Table 1:   Real GDP growth in Singapore 1965–2010

Y-O-Y	% change	Q1	Q2	Q3	Q4
1965–1985	9.2				
1986–1997	8.6				
1998–2008	5.0				
2004	8.7				
2005	6.6				
2006	8.7				
2007	8.2				
2008	1.4	7.3	2.8	0.1	−4.2
2009	−2.0	−9.4	−3.1	0.6	4.0
2010		16.9	19.3[1]		

Q-O-Q SA	Annualized % change	Q1	Q2	Q3	Q4
2007		11.4	7.1	7.6	−0.2
2008		17.2	−11.3	−4.1	−15.2
2009		−7.1	16.2	11.5	−2.8
2010		45.9	26.0[1]		

Note: [1] provisional.
Source: Department of Statistics (2009a), Table A1.1, A1.2, Monetary Authority of Singapore (2010), Ministry of Trade and Industry Press Release, 14th July 2010.

Table 2: Changes in employment by sector and the unemployment rate, Singapore 2007–2009

Thousands	Total	Manufacturing	Construction	Fin&Bus services	Other services[1]	Unemployment rate SA %[2]
2007	234.9	49.3	40.4	63.5	79.6	2.1 (3.0)
2008	221.6	19.5	64.0	47.6	88.8	2.2 (3.2)
Q1	73.2	11.8	14.5	16.4	30.1	1.9
Q2	71.4	10.1	22.4	17.5	20.8	2.2
Q3	55.7	4.6	16.5	12.0	22.3	2.3
Q4	21.3	−7.0	10.7	1.7	15.6	2.5
2009p	38.80	−43.0	25.2	16.2	39.9	3.0 (4.3)
Q1	−6.2	−22.1	8.3	0.3	7.2	3.3
Q2	−7.7	−15.9	4.7	2.0	1.8	3.3
Q3	14.0	−6.4	7.4	4.5	8.2	3.4
Q4	37.5	0.7	4.6	9.5	21.9	2.1

[1] All other service producing industries.
[2] Figure in brackets is the resident unemployment rate.
Source: Department of Statistics (2009a), Ministry of Manpower website www.mom.gov.sg, Monetary Authority of Singapore (2010a).

Table 3: Contribution to Singapore's real GDP growth by sector 2007–2009

%	Total[1]	Manufacturing	Construction	Fin&Bus services	Other services[2]
2007	8.2	1.6	0.6	2.9	2.7
2008	1.4	−1.1	0.7	1.7	1.7
Q1		3.1	0.4	3.0	2.7
Q2		−1.4	0.7	3.4	1.9
Q3		−2.9	0.9	1.8	1.9
Q4		−2.7	0.9	−0.3	−0.4
2009	−2.0	−1.0	0.7	0.2	−1.2
Q1		−6.2	0.9	−0.6	−2.8
Q2		−0.1	0.7	−0.3	−3.0
Q3		1.8	0.5	0.2	−1.7
Q4p		0.5	0.6	1.6	1.1

[1] Note that not all sectors are included so they do not sum to the Total column.

[2] All other service producing industries.

Source: Department of Statistics (2009a).

despite a slowing US economy and tighter credit conditions in global financial markets. Indeed, the expectation was that GDP growth in the Republic would slow in 2008 but 4–6% was still achievable even if there were a downturn in developed economies. Strength in some sectors of the economy, such as marine engineering and construction, which were more insulated from a US downturn, would prevent Singapore from sliding into a deep downturn. Other industries, such as tourism and transport-related hub services would also benefit from relatively resilient regional demand, at least in the short-term.

If there was a problem on the horizon, it was from rising consumer price inflation and domestic costs (Table 4). CPI inflation increased markedly in the first two quarters of 2008 as a result of both external and domestic cost pressures. Global oil and food prices had soared, while at home, wages and rental costs had risen in tandem with a tightening of the labour and commercial property markets. At the time, headline inflation was generally forecast to come in at the upper range of 4.5–5.5% for 2008 as a whole and, in fact, turned out to be 6.6%, significantly higher than the 2.1% in

Table 4:   Changes in prices and costs, Singapore 2007–2010

% change	CPI (2009 = 100)	ULC (2000 = 100)	UBC in manufacturing (2000 = 100)	Nominal earnings growth
2007	2.1	5.9	2.5	6.2
2008	6.6	8.3	10.4	5.4
Q1	6.6	7.2	3.9	10.6
Q2	7.5	6.0	12.3	3.1
Q3	6.6	9.8	13.1	5.5
Q4	5.4	10.2	12.6	2.4
2009	0.6	−0.1	−5.1	−2.6
Q1	3.4	10.2	9.3	−3.7
Q2	0.2	1.1	−8.3	−2.2
Q3	−0.3	−5.0	−11.8	−3.0
Q4	−0.8	−6.8	−9.1	−1.6
2010 Q1	0.9	–	–	–

Source: Department of Statistics (2009a), Monetary Authority of Singapore (2010), Ministry of Manpower website www.mom.gov.sg.

2007, and there was even a possibility of 'stagflation', every central banker's nightmare, if prices continued to rise and output fell more sharply than anticipated.

By October 2008, the situation facing policy-makers in Singapore had changed dramatically. What had hitherto been a US sub-prime mortgage problem had escalated into a fully-blown global financial crisis with a concomitant acute contraction of liquidity and credit, necessitating unprecedented emergency counter-cyclical activities by governments in both the developed and developing world. Worse still, the global slowdown was beginning to impact the Asian region.

In Singapore the economy had continued to weaken throughout the year with negative fourth quarter Y-O-Y GDP growth and sequential contractions for every quarter except the first as the earlier contraction in industrial output spread to other sectors of the economy which had been quite resilient up to that point. Construction was the only sector not to shrink in the final quarter (Tables 1 and 3). On the other hand, CPI inflation appeared to have peaked by the end of Q2 as a result of a fall in crude oil prices and moderating global food price inflation and domestic cost pressures began to soften by the end of the year in line with domestic activity (Table 4), so the balance of risks had shifted away from rising inflationary pressures to concerns over much weaker economic growth. By October 2008 CPI inflation was expected to moderate to 2.5–3.5% in 2009, while economic growth was revised down from 4–5% to around 3%. In the event the inflation forecast would turn out to be overly pessimistic (actual would be 0.6%) and the outlook for growth in the economy substantially optimistic (actual would be –2.0%). The worst of the crisis was yet to come.

With hindsight, Singapore appears to have been relatively unscathed by the global crisis as far as the financial fallout is concerned. As in other parts of Asia, Singapore's domestic financial markets are dominated by commercial banks which had limited direct exposure to toxic assets and whose fundamentals were relatively strong when the crisis broke, based on conventional financial soundness indicators.[4] Moreover, interbank rates in Asia generally did not spike in the latter part of 2008 so the global tightening of credit did not materially disrupt the flow of short-run credit. This was partly due to the fact that interbank borrowing is a relatively small source of funding in this region and governments acted quickly to provide the necessary liquidity.

As the Asian Development Bank (2009a) puts it: it was more of a 'credit hiccup' than a 'credit crunch'. Share prices did fall in Singapore in 2008 (Figure 1) and Singapore's de facto sovereign wealth funds — Temasek Holdings and the Government Investment Corporation of Singapore (GIC) appear to have suffered losses on their investments in western banks,[5] but the impact on domestic

---

[4] According to the Asian Development Bank (2009a) Singapore's banks had loan to deposit ratios in excess of 80%, a low level of non-performing loans, high risk-adjusted capital adequacy ratios, local ownership was high with a strong domestic retail base and total assets were more than ten times equity and generally of high quality.

[5] Retail investors, including some elderly, were also hit by the failure of Lehman Brothers structured notes and there were suggestions that there had been some miss-selling in Singapore.

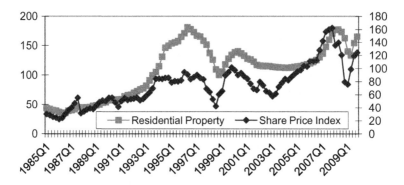

Figure 1: Singapore residential property and stock price indices.

Source: CEIC Database and IMF IFS Database.

household wealth was cushioned by unusually robust property prices which started to fall from the third quarter of 2008 until the second quarter of 2009, but then moved upwards again (Figure 1).

The financial impact of the crisis on Singapore was also cushioned by the fact that the fall in domestic non-bank loan growth, which occurred alongside the contraction in overall GDP, was less severe than during the Asian financial crisis of 1997–1998 and the 2001 downturn, due to strong demand for credit in the building and construction industry and from the residential housing sector.[6] As Figure 2 shows, total and business loan growth from the previous year did fall between Q4 2008 and Q3 2009 but consumer loan growth was quite resilient.

The impact of the global crisis on the 'real' economy was, however, much more dramatic as the slowdown in weighted GDP growth in Singapore's major trading partners (except China and India) fell from 4.6% in 2007 to 2.9% in 2008 and minus 0.8% in 2009 (Table 5). This transmitted the crisis to Asia through the trade channel. In contrast to

---

[6] Based on Monetary Authority of Singapore (2009b) estimates, the peak-to-trough decline in domestic banking units' non-bank loans was 0.8% between the third quarter of 2008 and the first quarter of 2009 compared to a 4.0% fall during the previous two crises.

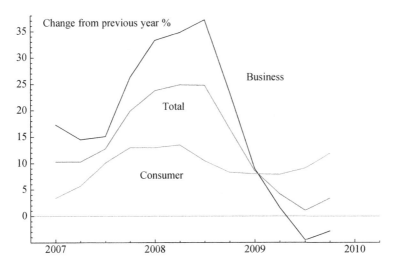

Figure 2:   Bank lending to non-bank customers 2007–2009.

Source: Monetary Authority of Singapore Financial Database, www.mas.gov.sg.

Table 5:   GDP growth in Singapore's trading partners 2007–2010[1]

Y-O-Y %	2007	2008	2009	2010f
Total	4.6	2.9	−0.8	4.2
Industrialised countries	2.2	0.3	−3.5	2.2
USA	2.4	0.0	−2.4	3.2
Eurozone	2.0	0.5	−4.1	1.2
Japan	1.9	0.5	−5.2	2.2
NIEs[2]	5.0	3.4	−1.8	5.1
ASEAN-4[3]	5.7	4.7	−0.4	5.3
China	10.7	8.8	8.7	9.9
India	8.2	7.2	6.4	8.1

[1] Groups are weighted by shares in Singapore's non-oil domestic exports.

[2] Hong Kong, Korea, Taiwan.

[3] Indonesia, Malaysia, Thailand and the Philippines.

Source: Monetary Authority of Singapore (2009a, 2009b, 2010).

the Asian financial crisis, when the developed countries were still growing above trend, in the recent crisis both Asia and the G3 experienced a synchronized downturn as exports and manufacturing collapsed and firms ran down inventories.[7] Due to the extraordinarily high degree of openness of the Singapore economy to international trade and capital flows the Republic was severely hit by the fall in its non-oil domestic exports, including electronics, by almost 8% in 2008 and 11% in 2009, compared to positive 2.3% growth in 2007 (Table 6). Moreover, in peak-to-trough terms, Singapore's merchandise exports declined by about 30% in the current crisis, compared to 10% and 13% in the 1998 and 2001 downturns, respectively.[8]

Table 6: Non-Oil domestic exports by selected destination 2007–2009

Y-O-Y % chg	2007	2008	2009
Total	2.3	−7.9	−10.6
Electronics	−9.2	−11.7	−18.0
G3	1.5	−41.8	−59.6
NIEs[1]	1.2	−11.2	11.6
ASEAN-3[2]	3.7	−18.5	−55.1
China	0.7	−2.3	−7.7

[1] Hong Kong, Korea, Taiwan.
[2] Indonesia, Malaysia, Thailand.
Source: Department of Statistics (2009a).

---

[7] According to the World Trade Organization in March 2009 global merchandise trade was set to contract by 9% in 2009, the first decline since 1982.

[8] Asian exports were especially sensitive to the fall in global GDP. See Holland *et al.* (2009). Singapore's exports were also dragged down by a sharp fall in intra-East Asian exports, especially those to China in electronics parts and components, compared with the downturn in 2001, when the G3 markets accounted for a larger share of the decline. This follows from the stronger synchronicity in trade among East Asian economies over the past few years as production and trade are increasingly linked via complex cross-border production networks, with China as a dominant assembly hub, driven by a common end-demand in developed economies. As a result, a collapse in demand in end-markets is transmitted swiftly across all member countries involved in the different stages of the production process, leading to a concerted collapse in trade (Monetary Authority of Singapore, 2009a).

Not surprisingly, in the fourth quarter 2008, Singapore's real GDP fell by 15.2% in annualized sequential terms and by 4.2% year-on-year, bringing full year growth to 1.4%, compared with 8.2% in 2007 and an average of 8% in the previous four years (Table 1).

Allowing for the usual time lags, in 2009 total employment contracted by 6.2% and 7.7% in the first two quarters, the first job losses since the SARS crisis, and the headline unemployment rate reached 3.4% in September (Table 2). From a longer run perspective, however, the labour market appears to have been more resilient during this recession with employment falling later in the cycle and rebounding earlier. Overall employment fell by 13,900 over only two quarters compared to 42,100 and 79,500 net job losses, respectively, during the Asian financial crisis and 2001 recession which persisted for at least one year.[9]

Moreover, *local* employment actually expanded with 41,800 more people in employment in 2009 compared to 1,300 in 2001 and a fall of 27,700 in 1998. Taking 2009 as a whole and despite the recession, strong job creation in the last two quarters, excluding manufacturing, resulted in positive employment growth for the economy as a whole (Table 2). Although the headline unemployment rate reached 3.4% in the third quarter, by the end of the fourth quarter it had fallen to 2.1%, substantially quicker than during the previous two downturns, such that it was almost back to its pre-crisis level.

Part of the reason for the resilience this time round is that the labour market was supported by stronger job creation in the construction and services sectors, including a number of long-term projects that were committed prior to the downturn.[10] This is in sharp contrast to the Asian financial crisis and the 2001 downturn when the construction sector was in the doldrums.

In addition, the impact on the labour market was cushioned by government initiatives to stem retrenchments, particularly amongst

---

[9] See Monetary Authority of Singapore (2010, p. 30).

[10] These include the integrated resorts (IRs) and the MRT Downtown Line, which generated strong demand for construction workers throughout the current recession and, together with the scheduled completion of new shopping malls, increased hiring in the services industries, such as retail trade and hotels & restaurants.

professional Singaporeans, including a S$4.5 billion Jobs Credit Scheme in the January 2009 budget. Meanwhile, firms themselves delayed the decision to trim headcount by taking advantage of Singapore's flexible work practices,[11] especially in the manufacturing sector, by placing a greater proportion of workers on shorter work-weeks or temporarily laying them off than during past recessions. Wages were also cut aggressively during this downturn (Figure 3), especially in services and in the public sector, including a reduction in the salaries of senior civil servants by up to 19% at the beginning of 2009 and the cancellation of mid-year bonuses.[12] As a result,

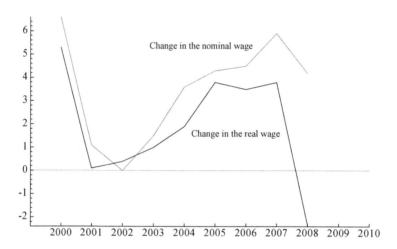

Figure 3:   Changes in nominal and real wages 2000–2008.

Source: Ministry of Manpower (2009b).

---

[11] As much as 84% of the workforce in the private sector in Singapore was under some form of flexible wage arrangement by end-2008, which includes variable monthly wage components and bonuses linked to key performance indicators. Public sector pay is also linked to the performance of the economy.

[12] Seasonally adjusted wages (which exclude employers' CPF contributions) fell by 6.2% from their peak in the first quarter of 2008, compared to 1.1% during the Asian Financial Crisis and 4.5% during the 2001 downturn. Moreover, wage adjustments in Singapore have been relatively larger than those in Japan, Hong Kong and Thailand (Monetary Authority of Singapore, 2009b).

nominal earnings growth slowed to 2.4% in the last quarter of 2008 and fell for all quarters in 2009 (Table 4), the first time earnings have fallen for four consecutive quarters on a year ago basis. For 2009 as a whole nominal earnings fell by 2.6% compared to rises of 5.4% and 6.2% for the two previous years and, according to a Ministry of manpower press release on the 16th March 2010, earnings also fell in real terms by 3.2%.

By early 2010, the global economy appeared to have averted a worst-case scenario and financial conditions began to stabilise, in large part due to unprecedented government intervention worldwide.[13] According to the IMF global GDP had returned to its previous peak by the fourth quarter of 2009. The thawing of credit markets, coupled with the improvement in investor sentiment, triggered a recovery in many asset markets, including in Singapore, as early as April 2009, helped by renewed liquidity flows into the region, including a resurgence of foreign interest in Singapore's equity market (Figure 1).

The 'real' rebound in Singapore was not to come until the second and third quarters of 2009 as firms replenished inventories and industrial output picked up following the recovery in investor sentiment and improvement in credit and financial market conditions. Quarter-on-quarter seasonally-adjusted annualised growth was 16.2% and 11.5% and Y-O-Y growth turned positive at 0.6% and 4.0% in the third and fourth quarters, respectively. This followed four consecutive quarters of sequential contraction and a cumulative output loss of 9.5% (Table 1).

---

[13] In October 2008, the 3-month US$ Libor-OIS spread, an indicator of risk and liquidity conditions, spiked to over 360 basis points amidst widespread panic following Lehman Brothers' collapse. However, the spread had fallen to around 40 basis points by June 2009 as liquidity conditions returned to normalcy. According to the June 2009 Merrill Lynch Global Fund Manager Survey, investor sentiment reached a turning point in the second quarter of 2009, with the majority of fund managers overweighting equities for the first time since December 2007. This time around, investors focused their portfolios around optimism over Asia's growth, including Singapore (Monetary Authority of Singapore, 2009a).

However, the widely expected severe and prolonged contraction did not materialize. By April 2010, Singapore had recovered all the output lost since the peak in the first quarter of 2008 so the recovery this time round has been stronger than in the last two downturns (Monetary Authority of Singapore, 2010). Recovery in the domestic economy became firmly rooted in the last quarter of 2009 following improving conditions in the global environment and the return of private sector demand just as government support was beginning to be removed and the earlier inventory bounce in worldwide manufacturing began to recede. World trade volumes rebounded[14] and global GDP returned to its previous peak as the G3 exited the global recession in the second half of 2010 and the industrialized countries looked set for positive growth in 2010 (Table 5). In fact, excluding volatile pharmaceutical output, Singapore experienced its third consecutive quarter of strong growth which has continued into the first quarter of 2010. In April 2010, the January official growth forecast for 2009 was confirmed at −2% and the 3–5% forecast for 2010 was revised up to 7–9%. In July the Ministry of Trade and Industry revised upwards the growth figures for the first quarter and the forecast for 2010 became 13–15%. Once again the Singapore economy has confounded the pessimists!

Meanwhile, headline CPI inflation year on year stabilized at about −0.6% in the second half of 2009, substantially below the first quarter figure of 3.4% and came out at 0.6% for the year as a whole (Table 4) in line with weaker global commodity prices and a softening of domestic business costs in tandem with the economic downturn, nominal wage adjustments and subsidies under the Jobs Credit Scheme. In the first quarter of 2010 consumer price inflation turned positive at 0.9% as the lagged effects of global price rises, especially energy, now filtered through into the Singapore economy.

---

[14] According to the Monetary Authority of Singapore (2010), and based on IMF data, world trade volume in December 2009 was just 10% below its previous peak of April 2008.

POST-CRISIS CHALLENGES FOR THE SINGAPORE ECONOMY

The post-crisis landscape will pose many challenges to Singapore but also offer opportunities. New drivers of growth will emerge but the risk of financial and other stresses in the global and regional environment still remain.

Over the longer term, Singapore is well-positioned, being at the heart of the Asian dynamo with China and India rising and creating huge new opportunities. But prudent policy making must focus on preparing for the worst especially in a small and highly open economy, such as Singapore. At least for the next five years or so, Singapore should prepare itself for a volatile environment and the occasional shock. First, financial stresses are not over in the more advanced countries, particularly if the debt crisis in Europe continues to impact on the real economy, while emerging Europe remains under stress.

Second, while massive policy responses have averted a global depression, the costs of policy are now likely to become more apparent. There could be higher risks of inflation in some countries while in others, the huge rise in public debt will undermine fundamentals and create other problems. The need to find funding for agencies such as the FDIC will create headwinds to growth or outright financial market shocks.

Third, with labour markets set to remain weak, free market ideologies discredited and populist forces unleashed, there could be new forms of protectionism, greater intrusive regulation of the private sector and other measures which could hurt Singapore. For example, further pressure from OECD countries to tighten up on tax havens and penalize countries which do not comply with changes in climate change policies. Fourth, the major currency realignments needed to re-balance the global economy have yet to take place. Moreover, we are witnessing a period when the dominance of the US as a global superpower will diminish gradually and a less straightforward multipolar geo-political balance will take its place. This may be a good thing in the long-run but the process of getting there is fraught with danger. For one thing, as the US changes from being a relatively benign hegemon into a more inward-looking power, it may lack the resources or inclination to step in and resolve global crises in the way that it used to, so we could see more global instability as a result.

The global economy is also likely to experience slower growth as oil prices rise in the longer run in response to supply and demand. This means that businesses will have to adjust to a permanently higher cost of energy and transportation and during the transition growth will be slower. Fiscal deficits will have to be brought down, which means a fiscal drag for some years in many countries, including the US, Europe and Japan. Household savings rates must rise in the US, the UK and other countries in Europe, limiting consumer spending as a driver of growth. In the meantime, banks will remain constrained and the disappearance of the shadow banking system will not be quickly replaced.

There will be important changes in global business strategy. MNCs may decide to focus, not so much on locations where there are low costs of production, but more on countries with large domestic markets or re-arrange their supply chains closer to home. Higher transportation costs and diminishing growth prospects in the G3 could also prompt MNCs to look for more cost-efficient production sites to build products for more price-sensitive Chinese, Indian and other emerging markets.

The prospects for Singapore's regional hinterland are also likely to be mixed. Whilst a resurgent Indonesia will create new opportunities for Singapore's regional hub, unless the political crisis in Malaysia is quickly resolved, tensions there are likely to intensify and have substantial political and economic effects on Singapore. Thailand is also experiencing unsettled political conditions limiting its economic upside. Patterns of regionalization could also change. Top-down regionalization efforts, such as the Asean Free Trade Area (AFTA) and ASEAN Economic Community (AEC), are likely to expand but it is not clear how effective these will be. The net effect will probably be positive but not very substantially so. On the other hand, sub-regional integration could become more important. The Greater Mekong Sub-Region is expanding and the

Iskandar Region in southern Malaysia is likely to have reached some sort of critical mass.

The structure of competitiveness will change as well. China will have no choice but to shift to a more flexible exchange rate regime with progressive liberalization of its balance of payments capital account. This will allow other Asian currencies to appreciate as well. At the same time, China will move up the value chain, opening up new opportunities for low-cost countries, such as Vietnam, Cambodia and Bangladesh but will also compete more aggressively in niches currently occupied by Malaysia, Thailand and, to a lesser extent, Singapore. In services, Chinese cities, such as Shanghai will move into a much higher economic league as financial centers, and will begin to compete head-on with Singapore and Hong Kong. Meanwhile, Indian manufacturing will become more competitive and will expand its global footprint. The good news is that Indian manufacturing will likely extend supply chains into Southeast Asia to benefit from manufacturing clusters in places such as Kulim in Penang and Bangkok's Eastern Seaboard which will thus remain globally competitive. But Indian manufacturing will also compete more with Southeast Asian economies.

SINGAPORE'S ECONOMIC STRATEGY[15]

Singapore's development strategy since independence in 1965 has always stressed the importance of maintaining rapid economic growth as a key barometer of its success, to provide the resources necessary for further growth and to redistribute some of the fruits of growth to Singapore's citizens, both in the short-term and, crucially, for retirement. Compulsory savings are to be mobilized through the Central Provident Fund (CPF) system, budget surpluses and the accumulation of official foreign exchange reserves earned through balance of payments surpluses. Meanwhile, private investment, much

---

[15] For some background on Singapore's economic history and economic strategy, see Lim Chong Yah *et al.* (1988), Peebles and Wilson (1996, 2002), Ghesquiere (2006).

of it foreign owned, is to be supplemented by extensive government investment in physical and social infrastructure. Although investment has fallen in the last few decades as a ratio of GDP, Singapore remains one of the highest gross savers in the world at around 50% of GDP.

Singapore has never been a laissez-faire economy since independence. Quite the opposite, economic policy-making has always been heavily interventionist and 'top-down'. In most countries this would have spelled disaster but, at least until recently, it has been remarkably successful as measured by conventional development indicators.

Singapore's economic system has been described as 'authoritarian capitalism' but it might be more accurately described as 'pragmatic socialism'. The government does not implement radical socialist redistribution policies through high taxes on higher earners or on corporate profits to generate revenues for the provision of universal social welfare benefits. Rather it has sought to benefit the general population through 'supply-side socialism' in the form of job creation, the provision of public housing, education and medical services. Sources of finance other than high taxes on earned incomes have been used for the provision of social services, including compulsory private savings and budget surpluses which are, themselves, the product of sustained growth in GDP over successive decades. Following the Land Acquisition Act of 1966 the government progressively secured land for public purposes to ensure that the rents were 'socialised' so that over 90% of land in Singapore is now owned by the government which leases it back for residential, commercial and industrial development.

Crucial to understanding Singapore's growth strategy is the role the government has played as 'entrepreneur' in the sense of establishing organisations necessary to support economic growth. In the mid-1960s Singapore had already developed an indigenous manufacturing sector of sorts in areas such as tin smelting, building materials and consumer goods to complement its earlier experience in commerce and trade, but the government was under some political pressure to deliver jobs quickly especially after the premature exit of the British from their bases. The manufacturing sector was, therefore, built up in the late 1960s by relying on foreign firms but large amounts of the necessary support was from government Statutory Boards including the Economic Development Board (EDB) which, since the mid-1960s has played the most important part in planning the development of the Singapore economy by attracting foreign investment and acting as a coordinating agency with other public sector bodies to ensure that they respond to the needs of foreign investors.

Other prominent Statutory Boards which still exist today are the Jurong Town Corporation (JTC) which was able to offer ready-built factories or prepare land and associated infrastructure for those investors who required specific features in their factories; the public Utilities Board (PUB), the Port of Singapore Authority (PSA) and the Housing and Development Board (HDB). The latter has provided public housing in which over 80% of Singaporeans live and 95% of them own their flats. The Central Provident Fund (CPF) mobilised domestic compulsory savings and the Government of Singapore Investment Corporation (GIC), a private company wholly owned by the Ministry of Finance invests part of the official foreign exchange reserves abroad.

As well as Statutory Boards the government has relied on its own Government-Linked Companies or GLCs which are controlled through Statutory Boards or the Government's holding companies. It is difficult to establish their numbers exactly or their weight in the economy but they are influential in all sectors. The most important GLC is Temasek Holdings, the government's main holding company which invests part of the government's budget surpluses. Other important GLCs are DBSBank and the GIC. Temasek is, for example, the controlling shareholder in Singapore Airlines (SIA) and Singapore Telecommunications (SingTel), two of Singapore's best known companies.

Although there have been key changes in the substance of Singapore's economic strategy since independence there has also been a remarkable degree of continuity and this has undoubtedly been helped by the fact that since 1959 the government has been formed by one party — the People's Action Party or PAP — and from 1959 to 1990 it had one Prime Minister — Lee Kuan Yew. The

PAP rationalizes its economic strategy in terms of material success and the fact that the dominance of the PAP can be seen to reduce uncertainty as far as foreign investors are concerned since there is not going to be a change in government through which a populist, redistributive party gained power. Singapore's low risk rating and triple 'A' credit rating in international markets suggests that this has been achieved.

Singapore's economic growth model has been overwhelmingly driven by exports and supported by a commitment to free trade, regional integration and export promotion When Singapore unexpectedly left the Federation of Malaysia in 1965 and became an independent Republic, with no further guarantee of free access to the Malaysian market, import substitution was perceived to be unsustainable in an economy with such a small domestic market and dearth of natural resources so Singapore decided consciously to 'make itself useful to the world' by embracing free trade, regional integration and export-oriented growth. Compared to most post-colonial developing countries at the time this was quite unusual.

Singapore has been an ardent advocate of multilateral trade liberalization through the General Agreement on Tariffs and Trade and its successor the World Trade Organization (WTO)[16] but, at the same time, has pursued regional trade integration, primarily through the Asia Pacific Economic Cooperation Forum (APEC), the Association of South-East Asian Nations (ASEAN) and was instrumental in launching the Asean Free Trade Area (AFTA) in the early 1990s. More recently, Singapore has negotiated bilateral preferential trade agreements with a large number of countries, including the USA, Australia, and Japan.[17]

There is no doubt that the extraordinary openness of the Singapore economy has meant that its growth cycle can be significantly affected by swings in external demand, such as during the

---

[16] It was no coincidence that Singapore was chosen to host the inaugural meeting of the WTO in 1996.

[17] For an update on the many trade agreements that Singapore has negotiated, see www.iesingapore.gov.sg.

Asian financial crisis of 1997–1998, in 2001 due to the sharp fall in global electronics demand and, of course, the drastic fall in exports as a result of the recent global financial crisis. With trade over three times its GDP Singapore is heavily dependent on imports of food, raw materials and energy, including water and its exceptionally high import content of exports means that one dollar of final expenditure sucks in approximately 64 cents of imports. On average, between 2006 and 2009, changes in external demand (exports) accounted for three-quarters of the changes in Singapore's real total demand, while changes in domestic demand accounted for a quarter (Department of Statistics, 2009a). This contrasts markedly with other industrialized economies such as Japan and the USA where domestic demand is the prime mover in total demand.

The strategy of export promotion combined with an insufficient supply of indigenous industrial entrepreneurs to fully employ the workforce made the attraction of foreign investment a top priority for Singapore. In contrast to most developing countries an 'open arms' policy towards MNCs and foreign labour was extended at a very early stage in the industrialization process. In 2008 Singapore still received about 4.8% of the total FDI inflow into developing countries and of the S$18 billion worth of domestic net investment commitments in manufacturing, 16 billion was foreign with large proportions for electronics, chemicals and biomedical manufacturing.

It is thus hard to overstate the importance of the role of private foreign resources in the economic development of Singapore and the notion that dependence on foreign multinationals and workers located in Singapore represents an Achilles heel has resurfaced in recent years. Indeed, since a large part of Singapore's GDP has always been produced by foreign companies and workers and so is not earned by Singaporeans, the Department of Statistics publishes its own unique concept of 'Indigenous GNP' (IGNP) which adjusts GNP to capture only those incomes which accrue to Singaporean citizens both from within and without Singapore. In 2008 the share of GDP that went to foreigners was 45%. Surprisingly, IGNP has rarely been a subject of discussion, let alone controversy. For the data,

see Department of Statistics (2009a) and Chapter 8 for its links with
fiscal policy.

The issue of foreign workers has also become much more controversial in the last two decades, especially during the present
global financial crisis and in the past the government has felt the
need periodically to remind Singaporeans of the importance of foreign labour to Singapore's economic growth. Growth accounting
estimates produced by the Ministry of Trade and Industry in 2001,
for example, purported to show that the contribution of foreign
labour was substantially above that of local labour, especially in the
1990s.[18]

To put this into some kind of perspective, according to the
Department of Statistics (2009b), the total population of Singapore
in 2009 was approximately 4.8 million, compared to 3 million in
1990. Over the same period the percentage of citizens fell from 86%
to 65%. While the total population grew at about 2.8% per annum on
average in the 1990s, Permanent Residents grew by almost 10%.
Between 2004 and 2009, these numbers were 3.3% and 8.1%, respectively. Perhaps more relevant to the present debate, the Ministry of
Manpower (2009b) calculates that, as of December 2009 64% of the
total labour force comprised 'locals' i.e., citizens and Permanent
Residents, which meant that non-local workers constituted about
35% of the workforce.

Although not obvious at first sight, macroeconomic policy in
Singapore has played a key part in Singapore's growth strategy.[19] It
has been characterized by high savings through the CPF and budget
surpluses, the application of prudent monetary and fiscal policies to
help establish Singapore as a premier financial centre and trading hub,
and a non-traditional monetary policy aimed at maintaining long-run
external competitiveness by keeping consumer price inflation low and

---

[18] *The Straits Times*, 1 November 2001, p. S 12.
[19] The role of the government in preserving the purchasing power of Singapore's
savings is one aspect of Singapore's 'citizen partnership for social equity' discussed in
detail in Chapter 11.

stable and attracting a continuous stream of mobile foreign capital and labour.

This strategy has been predicated to a large extent on the view that traditional monetary and fiscal policies are not very effective in Singapore compared to other countries, external demand is so important that there is little role for domestic demand as a countercyclical force, and exposure to a volatile global economy is a price worth paying for sustained economic growth.

It is well-known that fiscal policy is relatively ineffective as a stabilization tool in open economies with some flexibility in the exchange rate and high short-term capital mobility, but other factors come into play in Singapore. In particular, the ability to vary disposable income through changes in taxes or transfers is significantly reduced by the high compulsory contributions by employers and employees to the CPF and the very high marginal propensity to import considerably reduces the income multiplier effects on domestic income of any fiscal expansion or contraction. Singapore has, therefore, tended to use fiscal policy more as a longer-term device to mobilize resources for export-led growth, such as tax breaks to attract foreign MNCs, or for case-by-case social programs, such as encouraging families to have more children. The government does use fiscal policy to help recovery from downturns, such as in fiscal year 2009 when it ran an overall deficit of S$2.88 billion (Table 7), but one cannot escape from the feeling that there is reluctance to use the budget for serious countercyclical purposes on a regular basis as opposed to increasing surpluses as a source of saving for the future.[20] Challenges for fiscal policy are further discussed in Chapter 9 of this book.

From 1981 onwards, monetary policy in Singapore has essentially been exchange rate policy, whereby the Singapore dollar is

---

[20] This is made more difficult by the fact that under the present Constitution the government is not allowed to call on the reserves accumulated by previous governments unless the President approves. The FY2009 budget was the first time this had happened.

Table 7:   Fiscal position 2007–2009

S$ billion	2007	2008	2009[2]
Primary surplus/deficit[1]	7.39	3.00	−4.31
Overall surplus deficit	7.66	0.24	−2.88

[1] Before special transfers and net investment returns contribution.
[2] Revised from −10.20 and −8.67.
Source: Ministry of Finance (2009).

managed primarily to achieve low and stable domestic price inflation as the bedrock for sustaining export competitiveness and
inflows of mobile foreign capital and to enhance Singapore's reputa-
tion as a premier financial centre.[21] The impotence of 'traditional'
monetary policy or the targeting of interest rates or monetary
aggregates in Singapore follows largely from the high degree of
integration of Singapore's onshore financial markets with the rest of
the world which limits the central bank's ability to manipulate
domestic interest rates independent of the rest of the world and the
fact that Singapore is a classic price-taker in international goods
market so domestic prices are largely determined by global prices
multiplied by the exchange rate. Paradoxically, Singapore's central
bank — the Monetary Authority of Singapore (MAS) — has turned
this vulnerability into a virtue by taking advantage of the strong
pass-through of foreign into domestic prices by managing the
Singapore dollar exchange rate in such a way as to neutralize the
impact of imported inflation when necessary by intervening in
the foreign exchange market to appreciate the currency. The rationale behind Singapore's monetary policy is discussed in more detail
in Chapter 8.

Not surprisingly, given the perceived impotence of traditional
macro-stabilization policies combined with a vulnerability to
external shocks, traditional macroeconomic tools of demand management have often been supplemented by less conventional

---

[21] Singapore's monetary policy is discussed in more depth in Chapter 8 and exchange
rate policy in Chapter 10.

measures, including the bringing forward of public construction projects as a countercyclical measure when external demand falls (as in 2009), varying the supply of land released to private developers to stabilize the property market and the cutting back on imported labour on short-term contracts as a stabilization device when unemployment rises. The flexibility of the labour market, where a substantial portion of wages is dependent on the performance of the economy, is crucial to restore cost competitiveness since if costs in Singapore appear to be moving significantly out of line with its competitors, then direct action to reduce the real exchange rate by cutting costs is preferred to a large currency depreciation which might shake confidence in the currency, lower the value of savings, and would anyway only provide a transitory improvement in competitiveness until import price rises are passed on to domestic prices and wages. In 1999, a package of cost cuts lowered utility charges and the employer rate of contribution to the CPF was reduced. In the 2009 budget the CPF contribution rates were maintained in favour of employment subsidies to encourage employers to retain, or even increase their hiring of Singaporean workers. This 'Jobs Credit Scheme' was equivalent to a 9% cut in the employer contribution rate (Monetary Authority of Singapore, 2009b).

The flexibility of the Singapore system and the extent of public sector involvement mean that off-budget changes can be introduced quickly. There has been no attempt to construct a permanent social security system or to make the budget respond automatically to downswings to help the unemployed but they have benefited from a whole range of subsidies, rebates and ad hoc assistance provided on a discretionary basis during downturns.

The weakness of traditional macroeconomic policies, the smallness of the domestic market and the susceptibility of the economy to swings in external demand have all, therefore, reinforced the government's view that a certain amount of volatility in GDP growth is inevitable for Singapore. Similarly the government has always worried about its dependence on external demand and its ability to compete internationally in a dynamic world but the traditional response has been to retain the stress on exports but to 'diversify, restructure and upgrade'.[22]

After the 1985–1986 recession, for example, there was a perception that Singapore was losing comparative advantage in low skill labor-intensive goods and some capital-intensive goods relative to its competitors, but had not yet reached the stage at which it could compete with the industrial developed countries in skill-intensive goods. The narrowness of its production base therefore left Singapore vulnerable to the threat of de-industrialization or the "hollowing out" of the manufacturing sector as domestic costs rise and MNCs are tempted to re-locate their plants to lower wage economies.

One policy response was to 'grow a second wing' or encourage Singaporean firms to venture abroad in order to provide an extra source of income to the home economy from repatriated earnings to counterbalance any shortfall in export earnings. Prominent early initiatives included an industrial park in Suchou in China, an information technology park in Bangalore, and the establishment of hotels and port facilities in Vietnam.

Similar arguments were used to speed up the globalization of Singapore's financial sector and further integration into the world economy in the late 1990s, a strategy which encouraged Singapore's local banks to form global alliances and compete on the world stage. The result was a comprehensive set of reforms after 1997 to promote Singapore as a full service international financial centre. These included further widening of the scope for investment of CPF funds by increasing investment limits on unit trusts, the lifting of fixed commissions in the stock broking sector, a speeding up of the development of the domestic asset management industry by increasing the range of retirement products and allocating more government assets to selected fund managers located in Singapore, and a more proactive attempt to develop the local debt market.

---

[22] Upgrading the labour force through government subsidized, but market-based, training programmes has been a consistent feature of Singapore's labour market strategy to keep Singapore competitive in a dynamic world economy. For details on this, see Chapter 5.

Ironically, expanding into the Asian region in the 1990s, made Singapore more vulnerable to the slowdown in Asian markets during the Asian financial crisis of 1997–1998 and this prompted a need to diversify away from Asia. In January 2000 the Singapore Trade Development Board (now renamed International Enterprise Singapore) launched its Trade 21 plan which, amongst other things, encouraged local companies 'to sprout a third wing' by locating beyond Asia.

This coincided with the shift in trade policy towards negotiated bilateral preferential trade agreements with countries such as the USA, Australia, and Japan, whilst at the same time, continuing to press for further multilateral trade negotiations. Singapore has now signed a large number of such deals with a heterogeneous sample of countries, some of which do not seem to be very important in pure trading terms. The idea seems to be to make as many trading friends as possible and to use the agreements as a platform for wider cooperation in investment and other matters, and to use them as a 'carrot and a stick' to persuade other countries to join and thus eventually to converge on multilateral free trade.

The constant need to 'restructure' and 'upgrade' has always been an integral part of Singapore's economic policy-making. After the 1985 recession, the question was whether Singapore could shed some of its lower quality manufacturing, such as textiles and labour-intensive electronics and focus more on higher value-added manufacturing and services. In the 1990s, instead of relying exclusively on Singapore as a manufacturing production base and export platform for MNCs, the goal was now to broaden the manufacturing and service base into a 'total business center' providing conference facilities and industrial estates as self-contained business centers, to entice MNCs to use Singapore as their regional headquarters or produce high value-added exports and financial and business services. Certain clusters of activity such as chemicals, electronics, logistics and supply-chain management, healthcare and headquarters activities were earmarked for promotion.

This continued in the late 1990s and into the present decade with the vision to turn Singapore into an advanced globally-competitive knowledge-intensive innovative economy. Incentive schemes such as a Skills Development Fund and Promising Enterprise Programme were aimed at encouraging local talent and persuading successful Singaporean *émigrés* to return or at least 'network' with the mother country and foreign graduate schools were attracted to the Republic. Science parks of various kinds are sprouting up, such as Biopolis that will specialize in providing homes for firms and researchers in the field of life sciences as the latest incarnation of this longstanding policy.

Singapore's economic strategy may be a little unorthodox, but it has certainly been successful. In 2009, Singapore was 7th in the world ranked by GDP per capita (United Nations, 2009). Growth was most rapid between 1965 and 1985 but was not much slower from the mid-1980s up to the Asian financial crisis in 1998 (Table 1). However, real GDP growth appears to have slowed in the last decade.

Singapore's growth cycle has also become more volatile over time, especially with respect to the global electronics cycle. Between 1965 and 2000, there were only two years of falling output: in 1985–1986 and in 1998. Since then swings in output have been more frequent with the recession in 2001, the SARS crisis in 2003 and the recent financial crisis. As external demand accounts for approximately three-quarters of total final demand and Singapore's business cycle is highly correlated with external fluctuations (Monetary Authority of Singapore, 2009a), the problem arises primarily from the dependence of Singapore's growth on growth in external demand. The sectoral fluctuations of some clusters of industries in Singapore are more intrinsically linked together than others, such as IT-based industries and externally-oriented services but there is no sector or industry which is completely sheltered. In terms of employment turnover, the most volatile sectors are construction, manufacturing and financial services.

Between 1965 and 1990, Singapore registered stable labour productivity 'catch-up' relative to the USA and Western Europe but since then the picture has become more volatile (Ketels *et al.*, 2009). Over the last decade the main sources of weak productivity growth appear to be in services industries, such as restaurants and real estate services, and in construction. In manufacturing, overall productivity has grown at only 1.4% but performance has varied widely across different sectors with stronger growth in electronics, pharmaceuticals and transport engineering.

Worrying is that in absolute terms Singapore's average productivity between 2006 and 2008 in manufacturing is only 63% of that in the US and is well behind countries such as Sweden and Japan; while in services is 58% that of the US and much lower than Japan and Hong Kong (Figure 4). In the retail sector, it is only 75% that in Hong Kong and one-third that of the US. In construction, productivity in Singapore is almost half that of the US and one-third that of Japan. The upshot is that the need to raise productivity growth in every sector of the economy is now a key priority and one of the recommendations of the Economic Strategies Committee to be discussed in the following section.

Singapore's growth has not been at the expense of macroeconomic stability. From 1980 to 2008, the average annual inflation rate was approximately 2%. Headline unemployment has been more cyclical with highs of 6% in the first quarter of 1986, 3.7% in the last quarter of 2001 and 4.8% in the third quarter of 2003, during the SARS epidemic, but on average it has been 2.5% between 1980 and 2008. Even during the global financial crisis it peaked at only 3.4%. From 1985 onwards, the balance of payments has been characterized by substantial overall surpluses averaging 8% per year, and a continuous accumulation of official foreign exchange reserves, averaging over 10% growth per year between 1980 and 2008. Moreover, Singapore has never been an important recipient of foreign aid or built up any significant official foreign debt.

From the broader welfare perspective, in the 2009 United Nations Human Development Index (United Nations, 2009) which is published in its annual Human Development Report, Singapore was ranked 23st in the world. This placed the Republic in the 'high' human development category. With a score of minus 16 for the

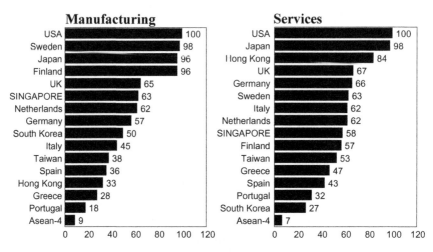

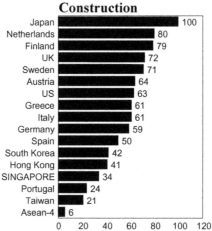

Figure 4: Cross-country productivity comparisons.[1]

[1] Average productivity levels 2006–2008

Source: Economic Strategies Committee, www.esc.gov.

difference between the ranking based on real GDP per capita and a rank of 21 in the HDI, this implies that Singapore was more 'advanced' in terms of income than in social development but this is not unusual and Singapore's welfare achievements when viewed from a more disaggregated perspective, such as the access of its people to housing, healthcare and education and the virtual elimination of absolute poverty and infant mortality, are impressive.[23]

More controversial has been Singapore's record in terms of income inequality. With a Gini coefficient of around 0.481 (0.462 after government taxes and transfers) Singapore ranks as an economy with relatively high income inequality (Ketels *et al.*, 2009), higher than in the vast majority of developed countries. Moreover, it has increased over the last decade, much more so than in other developed countries, as technological change benefits those with higher skills and knowledge and globalization increases the competition for jobs. Singapore's meritocratic education system may indirectly have reinforced this. Although all income groups of employed households have experienced growth in real incomes per household member over the last decade, it has been almost double for the top quintile compared to the bottom (Department of Statistics, 2008). However, public spending in Singapore, which disproportionately benefits those on lower incomes, may have cushioned some of the social implications of this process.

RE-THINKING SINGAPORE'S ECONOMIC STRATEGY

In view of the remarkable progress that has been made, to criticize Singapore's economic strategy, particularly within Singapore itself, sometimes feels like criticizing the International Red Cross. Nonetheless there are those who feel that the Republic's growth and welfare performance in the last two decades has fallen short of expectations and that it is time to re-think some of the basic tenets

---

[23] This can easily be ascertained from the welfare indicators published annually by the Asian Development Bank (2009b) where, curiously, Singapore is still classed as a developing country in the Asia-Pacific region. Only on energy and environmental matters does Singapore do badly, as do many developed countries, such as Japan and the US and emerging countries such as China.

of the strategy.[24] In particular, the highly centralized top-down role of government in terms of control over resources, such as land and the corporate sector; the centralized mobilization of savings through the CPF and the directing of investment through government departments into targeted areas; and the use of fiscal, education and labour market policies to create the environment to achieve these ends. Allied to this is the continued emphasis on export-led growth with foreign companies playing a dominant role and the target of keeping manufacturing at about 20–25% of GDP.

A key theme of the critics is that notwithstanding efforts to diversify, restructure and upgrade, Singapore has become too dependent on foreign resources. It may be desirable to have a GDP growth target but it must be *sustainable* in terms of Singapore's potential labour force and productivity growth and the technologies and innovation capacity the Republic can acquire at reasonable cost. Given the low fertility rate and already high investment ratio to GDP, Singapore can only achieve high growth rates of 6–7% with present levels of productivity and labour force participation by importing more foreign labour to increase employment. But foreign workers already account for 35% of the labour force and there is concern that social problems are beginning to manifest themselves from the rapid influx of foreign workers and the rise in the number of Permanent Residents who compete with citizens for housing, healthcare and education. Singaporeans are now, it is suggested, being crowded out of the

---

[24] In this section, we borrow from a largely eclectic literature, mostly based in Singapore, which shares the view that there should be a re-thinking of some of the objectives of economic policy in Singapore to aim for broader welfare goals and do more to build 'inherent capabilities' for indigenous workers and companies. Many of these views are articulated through feedback to local newspapers, such as the *Straits Times* and in blogs, including *theonlinecitizen.com*. For an example, see http://leongszehian.com. Some of these ideas were also consolidated by the Economic Society of Singapore Policy Feedback Sub-Committee in their submissions to the Economic Strategies Committee. See also Lim (2009) and Choy Keen Meng (2008).

property market, good schools and jobs. Immigration may, therefore have to be calibrated at a slower rate and the growth target reduced accordingly to around 3–5%.

There is also some doubt whether the 'trickle down' of the benefits of past growth has been sufficient to compensate for the sacrifices that Singaporean workers have made to keep the externally-oriented growth model working. Singapore's 'supply-side socialism' requires workers to accept wage cuts and temporary unemployment when the economy goes into recession in order to restore cost competitiveness and take the pressure off exchange rate adjustment and to keep mobile foreign capital in Singapore. If necessary, employer costs are reduced by cuts in the employer CPF rate borne by workers. Only during the latest recession was there an attempt to protect Singaporean workers through wage subsidies. The implicit deal, of course is that the cost adjustments will work quickly and employment and real wages will rise again as they have done in the past and some of the hardship will be alleviated through one-off transfer payments. The fundamental problem is that the benefits of growth may have become unevenly spread and this has contributed to the rise in income inequality.

Hence the suggestion that the objectives of economic policy should be widened away from a narrow focus on GDP growth to criteria which are more 'explicitly inclusive'.[25] It is well-known that GDP is a narrow measure of economic welfare, being more of an intermediate target than an end in itself, and it could be supplemented with indicators which are better proxies for improvements in citizen welfare, such as the real median wage, median household income or the ratio of the incomes of the bottom quintile of income earners to the top quintile.[26] At the same time, the monitoring of these welfare indicators might be accompanied by targets for income equality and other measures of the quality of life. Some would also like a widening of the differential between the benefits to citizens and

---

[25] Basant Kapur makes this point in Chapter 3.
[26] See for example Stiglitz *et al.* (2009).

the benefits to Permanent Residents to prevent the erosion of national identity and social cohesion.[27]

There is a more subtle issue here that Singapore may have become 'hooked' on cheap labour from abroad to sustain growth and, as a result, wages and productivity have been reduced, further exacerbating income differentials. Singapore has one of the highest inflows of unskilled and semi-skilled workers in recent years. The Foreign Worker Levy introduced in 1990 was supposed to make foreign workers as expensive as local workers but because it is fixed in absolute terms its impact has lessened over time. In other words, although foreign workers were supposed to complement local workers, particularly in high productivity jobs where local skills were lacking or in 'dirty' jobs which are shunned by Singaporeans, employers may now be using foreign workers as a means to keep local wages down across a wide range of occupations thus reducing wage growth for lower income deciles. This process has been reinforced by the increasing 'globalization' of these jobs and may have been inimical to productivity growth because employers have little incentive to economize on labour, raise capital intensity or reorganize production.

If the present growth model isn't working very well, then why not change it? A first step would be to reset the goals to encompass a moderate 3–5% growth in GDP (or GNP), reduce dependence on foreign workers, make growth 'more inclusive' and shift the emphasis more towards domestic demand and the services sector, rather than manufacturing for export. Being small may make this more difficult but other countries, such as Hong Kong and Switzerland, show that it can be done.

According to this perspective, inclusive growth would be based on increasing productivity through higher wages for resident workers by restricting the inflow of foreign workers. This might also help to improve income inequality and raise the ratio of domestic consumption

---

[27] The trick here is to improve on the system by adding some redistributive mechanisms without abandoning the principle of individual responsibility. For an example of this in the context of healthcare financing, see Chapter 7.

to income, which was 39.7% on average between 2005 and 2009 and is very low compared to other countries. This could also be achieved by cuts in the employee CPF contribution rate or a rise in the employer contribution rate and increasing consumer wealth by distributing shares in GLCs. A more radical proposal would be to make the tax and benefit system more redistributive.

A further step would be to change the mindset of the Civil Service away from incentives given to manufacturing for export and towards the creation of a 'heterogeneous and diversified' high value-added services sector with less stress on exports and more stress on generating domestic demand. Singapore has always had a high proportion of services in GDP due to its history as an entrepot trading port but these are still largely 'traditional' services related to transport and wholesale business activities. By contrast, Singapore's share of global 'modern services, such as those associated with financial and information technology is relatively small, so there is, it seems, some scope for further expansion.[28]

High-income services may, coincidentally, have properties which might help Singapore adjust to the ups and downs of the global business cycle: they tend to be less volatile than manufacturing and construction and more recession-proof in the sense that medical services, tertiary education and wealth management attract higher value-added buyers than manufactured electronics components destined ultimately for overseas mass market products. They might also generate more local employment (entertainment, fashion, grooming), particularly for Singaporeans who do not have the necessary human capital to work in MNCs and might otherwise migrate elsewhere; have larger 'spin-offs' on other sectors; be less import-intensive and could help to build up domestic demand and workers' incomes to reduce Singapore's dependence on external demand.

This challenges a key assumption that the domestic market and stock of human resources is too small to provide the necessary demand

---

[28] For the potential of services for Singapore, see Monetary Authority of Singapore (2009b) and Eichengreen and Gupta (2009).

and economies of scale to sustain more indigenous economic activity so that export-led growth supported by foreign labour and capital is the only feasible option. Similar arguments have been used to encourage the financial sector to expand globally due to the perceived lack of a critical mass for successful fund management and an insufficient supply of indigenous talent and innovation. Certainly the number of consumers is relatively small but in terms of purchasing power and the value of output Singapore is not a small player on the world stage.[29]

A further complaint stems from the overwhelmingly 'top-down' nature of economic policy in Singapore which is already saturated with a confusing array of overlapping institutions to pick winners, upgrade skills and technology, raise productivity and enhance innovation.[30] Singapore does not lack for expensive and capital-intensive infrastructure and a mentality of 'build-it and they will come'.

A crucial feature of Singapore's economic strategy has been high levels of gross national savings and investment and a concentration of savings in the hands of the government. In the past, one could justify such resource mobilization as part of a successful non-inflationary development strategy geared towards specific 'socialist' goals, including the spread of home ownership and sufficient savings to ensure external security. In effect, forced savings through the CPF mechanism were used to finance development infrastructure and public goods (port, airport, telecommunications, roads) whilst at the same time some of these savings were converted into a portfolio of foreign assets at the MAS and GIC to generate a diversified source of income from abroad. Singapore was thus able to finance development without recourse to deficit financing, foreign commercial debt, or foreign aid, whilst simultaneously achieving export-led growth based upon an efficient inflow of foreign direct investment.

---

[29] According to the World Bank (2009) rankings, Singapore lies 42nd in the world in terms of the level of GDP, one place behind Malaysia and above Pakistan and the Philippines.

[30] National Productivity Board or NPB (1972), Singapore Productivity and Standards Board (1996) merging the NPB and Singapore Institute of Standards and Industrial Research (1996), the Standards, Productivity and Innovation Board or SPRING (2002).

Of course provision has to be made for a slowdown in potential GDP growth and the ageing population and a rise in healthcare costs for the elderly, but it has become harder to justify the high level of savings, having already achieved the essential development infrastructure and given the opportunity costs in terms of private consumption and the over-centralization of savings and investment decisions. There have been large surpluses in the balance of payments, both on current account and capital account and a relentless accumulation of official foreign reserve assets. The debate in Singapore has also been complicated by the secrecy which surrounds the official foreign exchange reserves, the non-standard way in which the budget is presented and the fact that the precise returns on public savings and reserve assets are not public information.

Perhaps government should step back a little and allow more decentralized market forces to allocate resources, with less strategic help to foreign MNCs and more help to indigenous firms and 'home-grown entrepreneurs'. This would be less expensive, less intensive in land and energy, increase employment and create a 'more diverse corporate infrastructure' which could capitalize on Singapore's potential comparative advantage in environmental sustainability, energy conservation, urban solutions, and solutions for an ageing population, such as healthcare and financial services.

In international comparisons, Singapore appears to do well in overall measures of competitiveness but more in line with a highly-skilled version of the investment-driven model based on science related innovation, rather than creative and entrepreneurial-linked innovation.[31] In a recent competitiveness report by the Asia Competitiveness Institute (Ketels *et al.*, 2009) based on criteria developed at Harvard

---

[31] The criticism that Singapore has not generated sufficient 'quality growth', as opposed to input driven growth based on labour and capital inputs, is not new. In 1994, Paul Krugman (1994) categorized Singapore's growth over the preceding three decades as essentially input driven rather than the result of quality growth as proxied by total factor productivity growth (TFPG). The official Singapore view seems to be that TFPG has increased in recent decades as past investment in education and infrastructure bore fruit, but TFPG is notoriously difficult to measure and can be quite volatile over the cycle (Monetary Authority of Singapore, 2010).

University by Michael Porter,[32] Singapore does well on aspects of macroeconomic competitiveness which are directly controllable by government, i.e., the context in which companies operate, such as the effectiveness of its public institutions, but 'the controlled nature of Singaporean society might inhibit "creative" activities that tend to thrive in less-structured environments'.

In terms of microeconomic competitiveness, Singapore is also world class in terms of factor input conditions and rules and regulations affecting business and in innovation capacity has a strong mix of world-leading quality in education and research, but its performance on entrepreneurship is disappointing and its low level of domestic company sophistication is typical of an export-oriented economy dominated by foreign multinationals. There is also some concern about the strong role of GLCs. It is not that they perform badly, quite the opposite, they match the performance of their best private sector-owned peers, but 'there remains a question as to whether these GLCs are effective in existing markets but less nimble in pursuing entrepreneurial ventures in new fields'.[33] Taken together, MNCs and GLCs might help explain Singapore's relatively poor performance in entrepreneurship.

There are a number of ways in which Singapore might go forward if it accepts these criticisms. To begin with it could move away from the

---

[32] Porter himself (2001) has in the past chastised Singapore for its pursuit of an activist industrial policy, heavy government involvement in the economy, and attempts to 'pick winners', which has not fostered sufficient innovation. He suggested that the focus should shift much more towards services and creating the conditions for clusters' of activity to flourish, with stronger competition policies and more privatization of GLCs, and policies to create a more chaotic and heterogeneous society which is more flexible and tolerant of different groups of people with new ideas, tastes and beliefs.

[33] That GLCs might be a factor explaining Singapore's weakness in the microeconomic environment was also suggested by Cardarelli *et al.* (2000). In their view the intensity of local competition is the most important single variable in microeconomic competitiveness, especially the quality and network of domestic suppliers and related industries, since this competition acts as a training ground for international competition.

USA-style innovation-driven economy based on research into 'hard science' and a hub creating the next generation of global technologies towards an innovation-driven economy closer to Singapore's current competitive strengths as a knowledge-based hub with world class companies and a secure legal environment, perhaps identifying and commercializing opportunities where existing knowledge has not been fully applied. For example, it could export its expertise in public services from healthcare to city planning and public administration or capture some of the spin-offs from multinationals operating in the Republic.

Singapore could also diversify production away from the MNC 'monoculture' to a more balanced composition of local companies and MNCs and away from G3 markets, which may grow more slowly in future, towards the region and emerging markets. This might also increase Singapore's resilience to external shocks. MNCs have been useful in the past and will continue to play a role in the future but they have their own supply chains and partners which may become consolidated and relocated nearer to home as transportation costs rise, their currencies weaken and they want to protect their intellectual property rights.

Perhaps more effort could be put in to nurture globally competitive domestically-owned small and medium sized enterprises in manufacturing and services. Especially where there are complementarities and these firms can take advantage of an industrial hinterland as Hong Kong has done with regard to Shenzhen. Singapore's GDP *is large* and *it can* take advantage of economies of scale. One policy response would be to strengthen competition law so local SMEs are not excluded from opportunities.

Singapore could develop globally competitive savings-related local financial industries as in Hong Kong and Australia, such as private pension funds and fund management, which are presently hampered by weaknesses in the mobilisation and deployment of domestic savings which are often channelled through government agencies and Sovereign Wealth Funds (SWFs) and much are invested outside Singapore. This would also provide some diversification advantages. There are opportunities to build on Singapore's strength in fixed income assets and take advantage of regional demand.

Another suggestion is to 'revitalise regionalisation' on the assumption that Singapore has not made enough effort to integrate with its close neighbours in the region and take full advantage of opportunities to deepen economic integration in Singapore's hinterland. Singapore is an important investor in Malaysia, for example, and firms on both sides of the causeways linking the two countries have for some time been taking advantage of complementarities between the two locations, with Singapore firms establishing manufacturing operations in nearby Johor Bahru to take advantage of cheaper labour and land, and an evolving business-friendly infrastructure, whilst retaining their headquarters and research and development activities in Singapore.

The immediate focus would be on Malaysia and Indonesia but could stretch as far as Indochina. At the very least, the government should put more priority on improving bilateral relations with these countries, removing cross-border obstacles to trade and financial flows, be more pro-active in the funding of transportation and other infrastructure, such a high speed train service to the Malaysian capital Kuala Lumpur, and should invest in the Iskandar Development Region on Singapore's doorstep in the Malaysian State of Johor.[34]

The outcome would be to increase demand for Singapore's goods and services and provide economies of scale and resources, particularly land and labour, which can release valuable land in the Republic for higher value-added activities. It might also provide social infrastructure for leisure activities and retirement as Hong Kong has done in the Pearl River Delta of southern China. There might be more subtle benefits if Singapore can expand its services exports to the region and diversify the scope of these activities if this reduces fluctuations in output and employment since it seems that regional business cycles do not at present appear to have a strong influence on Singapore's domestic business cycle compared to the rest of the world (Monetary Authority of Singapore, 2009a).

---

[34] Recent progress in settling the issue of Malaysia's railway land in Singapore gives some grounds for optimism.

Moreover, there are some precedents. Singapore was a prime mover in the establishment in 1990 of an industrial park on the nearby Indonesian island of Batam as part of a 'growth triangle' linking Singapore, Johor and the Riau Islands in Indonesia. The idea was to pool economic resources in a complementary fashion to stimulate growth by combining cheap Indonesian land and labor with Singaporean infrastructure and management and financial services to produce labor-intensive manufactured goods. Activity has now been extended to other parts of the Riau, including Bintan, where light industries and tourism are promoted, and there is significant activity in shipyard and related activities and the petroleum industry dotted around the islands, such as Karimun.

THE ECONOMIC STRATEGIES COMMITTEE (ESC)

The ESC was set up in May 2009 to develop strategies for Singapore 'to build capabilities and maximize opportunities as a global city in a new world environment, so as to achieve sustained and inclusive economic growth'. It was chaired by the Finance Minister, Tharman Shanmugaratnam and included representatives drawn from government, the labour movement and the private sector. Its findings were released in February 2010.[35]

The ESC accepted (see Figure 4 above) that in a cross-country comparison Singapore's productivity in manufacturing and services, especially in the retail sector, falls well short of other countries, such as the USA, Japan and Sweden, and in construction is lower than Korea and Hong Kong. Reminiscent of the past, the Committee recommends that a high level national council be established to oversee and drive efforts to boost productivity, a National Productivity Fund to support productivity initiatives and a Productivity and Innovation Centre to act as 'a national productivity knowledge base'. The target is now 2–3% productivity growth per year to enable GDP to grow on average by 3 to 5% per year over the next

---

[35] The recommendations of the ESC can be found at www.esc.gov.sg.

decade. So growth expectations may be a little lower but institutionally-driven productivity growth to sustain GDP growth remains the key goal.[36]

As far as the past is concerned, the government's view[37] is that productivity drives have not failed. After all, productivity levels have doubled since 1980 and there has been an increase in TFPG. Other countries, such as the Irish Republic, have experienced rapid productivity growth but then it has fallen. Any attempt to sacrifice growth in order to reduce volatility by smoothing the cycle will simply reduce longer-run average growth, which would not increase income or jobs for less-skilled lower-income workers. It is true that growth was above potential between 2004 and 2008 but it was only 5% over the decade 1998 to 2008 as a whole so faster growth was needed to compensate for growth below potential in 2001 and during the SARS crisis.

According to this viewpoint, it is wrong, to say that the government was pursuing growth at all costs and that this resulted in lower incomes for low income earners due to an inflow of foreign workers putting downward pressure on local wages. On the contrary, foreign labour has enabled business to take advantage of growth which comes in waves, such as the 7–8 year cycle in petrochemicals, and is necessary to address supply bottlenecks in Singapore — to build the MRT, drive the buses, provide healthcare, etc. But yes a large part of GDP growth in the last decade was achieved through the expansion of the workforce, both resident and foreign, and it is not sustainable in the long-run given the demographics of the resident labour force and the over-reliance on foreign workers which might reduce the incentive to upgrade and raise productivity. This is an important shift in thinking.

The correct policy response, therefore, is to maximize the opportunities for all Singaporeans and not to reduce the incentive to work, but

---

[36] According to the Monetary Authority of Singapore (2010) 3 to 5% growth is possible over the next decade based on its own productivity growth estimates and the ESC assumption of a slower labour force growth rate of 1-2% per annum between 2010 and 2019.

[37] See, for example, Shanmugaratnam (2010).

this does not rule out help for low income families and a rise in government expenditures over the next 5–10 years. In addition the incomes of low-wage workers can continue to be enhanced through the Workfare Income Supplement Scheme introduced in 2007 and, crucially, the foreign workers' levy is to be raised gradually to ensure that dependence on the foreign workforce does not grow excessively. At the same time, the quality of the foreign workforce is to be increased by increasing the skilled levy differential.

As far as income inequality is concerned, official figures suggest that the median income per Singaporean household member grew between 2005 and 2008 and there was some growth in lower income household incomes, even if it was less than the median. Wages rose between 2006 and 2008 to offset the fall in wages of low income groups in the first half of the decade and unemployment has fallen since late 2003. Moreover, the Gini coefficient for other cities, such as Hong Kong and New York exceeds 0.5 and the Scandinavian model, which is often cited as an alternative for Singapore, is uniquely related to the historical development of a close-knit homogenous society accustomed to high taxes to subsidize middle and lower income households. So there doesn't seem to be a significant shift in thinking here.

On the face of it, the post-ESC strategy seems to be a continuation of the top-down, diversify and upgrade model. The aim is now to build a distinctive global city and an endearing home by attracting and nurturing diverse pools of talent, both home-grown and global, bring in top quality post-graduate institutions, reposition the Civic District as a premier arts and culture hub and make Singapore a location to 'pinnacle' international events in business, sports and culture. At the same time there will be an accelerated shift towards higher value-added and more land-efficient activities to rejuvenate mature industrial parks. While Singapore will not try to pick winners "we would need to identify emerging trends... to develop clusters, including a new waterfront city at Tanjong Pagar".[38] The government continues, therefore, to see its role essentially as 'an enabling one'. In

---

[38] Economic Strategies Committee www.esc.gov.sg.

view of the longstanding complaint by some that the Singapore government, directly or indirectly, influence all aspects of economic life in Singapore this seems to be a little understated.[39]

Yet there are some subtle changes of emphasis, including the desire to establish intelligent energy systems to increase energy efficiency and to diversify away from imports of coal and electricity, set up a liquefied natural gas terminal and to study the feasibility of using nuclear power.

The emphasis on export-oriented-MNC growth does not seem to have been abandoned in favour of a growth model substantially re-oriented towards domestic demand, but there appears to be more emphasis on building a stronger base of local companies. This fits in with the greater stress now being placed on SMEs in development organizations, such as the Asian Development Bank (2009a). The plan now is to develop a vibrant and diverse corporate ecosystem and a deeper base of globally-competitive local enterprises to grow the external wing of the economy, although "MNCs must remain key players in our economy". One useful innovation is to increase the supply of trade finance, as in other countries, through some sort of export-import bank or multipurpose export credit agency funded by government equity. Growth-oriented SMEs located in Singapore will also get help in the form of funding for new capital.

Similarly, it is not clear how far, if at all, the balance will shift away from capital-intensive manufacturing exports towards more domestic-oriented services and whether the emphasis is to be more on the region or the global economy. There will be renewed commitment to work towards an ASEAN Economic Community by 2015 and "our companies have an important window of opportunity to create a strong presence in Asia over the next 5 to 10 years". But as far as the

---

[39] As the ESC puts it "The government can help to catalyse economic restructuring. Raising productivity, and shifting to more efficient use of labour, land and energy will require changes in our economic structure. However, the government cannot prescribe which companies and sectors should grow. It should instead provide the right price signals (e.g., foreign worker levies) and enable market forces to reallocate scarce resources to where they can be most profitably used".

G3 markets are concerned "Singapore should stay engaged in these markets, and grow its role over the next decade as a key global centre for high value manufacturing and services".

Manufacturing it seems will remain at 20 to 25% of GDP but with more stress on design-driven innovation and targeted high value-added areas such as 'nutriceutals', bioelectronics and 'mission-critical components', such as medical devices. Research and development will be increased to 3.5% of GDP by 2015. On the other hand, attempts will also be made to integrate physical trade with manufactured-related services, including HQ related activities, R&D and intellectual property management and to establish Singapore as a location for 'future-ready' urban solutions, such as 'smart' transportation and energy efficiency and management. This is not exactly the domestic-demand, SME, local services-oriented strategy favoured by some economists but it does, at least, recognize that it is much harder to separate services from manufacturing in the modern world.

END NOTES

Asian Development Bank (2009a). *Asian Development Outlook 2009.* Manila: Asian Development Bank.

Asian Development Bank (2009b). *Highlights, Key Indicators for Asia and the Pacific.* 40th Edition, Manila: Asian Development Bank.

Cardarelli, R, Gobat, J and J Lee (2000). *Singapore: Selected Issues,* International Monetary Fund, Staff Country Report 00/83. Washington: International Monetary Fund.

Choy, Keen Meng (2008). *Singapore's Changing Economic Model, Management of Success Revisited: A Critical Survey of Modern Singapore.* Singapore: Institute of Southeast Asian Studies.

Department of Statistics (2008). *Key Household Income Trends, 2007.* Singapore: Department of Statistics, Occasional Paper on Income Statistics.

Department of Statistics (2009a). *Economic Survey of Singapore.* Singapore: Department of Statistics.

Department of Statistics (2009b). *Population Trends* 2009. Singapore: Department of Statistics.

Eichengreen, B and P Gupta (2009). *Two Waves of Service Sector Growth*. Washington: National Bureau of Economic Research, Working Paper W14968.

Ghesquiere, H (2006). *Singapore's Ascent: Engineering Prosperity Through Enlightened Strategy*. Singapore: Thomson Learning.

Holland, D and Associates (2009). The world economy: Asian economies are highly sensitive to the collapse of world trade. *National Institute Economic Review*, 2008(22), 22–25.

Ketels, C, Lal A and Neo Boon Siong (2009). *Singapore Competitiveness Report 2009*, Singapore: Lee Kuan Yew School of Public Policy Asia Competitiveness Institute.

Krugman, P (1994). The myth of Asia's miracle. *Foreign Affairs*, 73, November–December, 62–78.

Lim Chong Yah and Associates (1988). *Policy Options for the Singapore Economy*. Singapore: McGraw-Hill.

Lim, Linda (2009). Singapore's economic growth model — Too much or too little? *Ethos*, Issue 6, Singapore: Civil Service Commission.

Ministry of Finance (2009). *Review of Financial Year*. Singapore: Ministry of Finance.

Ministry of Manpower (2009a). *Survey on Annual Wage Changes*, 1980–2009. Singapore, Ministry of Manpower.

Ministry of Manpower (2009b). *Labour Market 2009*. Singapore, Ministry of Manpower.

Monetary Authority of Singapore (2009a). *Macroeconomic Review*. Volume VIII, Issue 1, April, Singapore: Economic Policy Department, Monetary Authority of Singapore.

Monetary Authority of Singapore (2009b). *Macroeconomic Review*. Volume VIII, Issue 2, October, Singapore: Economic Policy Department, Monetary Authority of Singapore.

Monetary Authority of Singapore (2010). *Macroeconomic Review*. Volume IX, Issue 1, April, Singapore: Economic Policy Department, Monetary Authority of Singapore.

Peebles, G and P Wilson (1996). *The Singapore Economy*. Cheltenham, UK: Edward Elgar.

Peebles, G and P Wilson (2002). *Economic Growth and Development in Singapore.* Cheltenham, UK: Edward Elgar.

Porter, M (2001). *The Competitive Advantage of Singapore: Transition to the Innovation Stage.* Presentation at the August 2001 New Economy Conference, Institute for Strategy and Competition.

Shanmugaratnam, T (2010). *Economic Growth Benefits and Citizens.* Singapore: Straits Times, 6 March.

Stiglitz, J, Sen, A and J Fitoussi (2009). *Report by the Commission on the Measurement of Economic Performance and Social Progress.* www.stiglitz-sen-fitoussi.fr/en/membres.htm.

United Nations (2009). *Human Development Report 2009.*

World Bank (2009). *World Development Indicators Database.* Washington: the World Bank.

Chapter 3

ECONOMIC POLICY-MAKING IN SINGAPORE: SOME REFLECTIONS

Basant K Kapur

INTRODUCTION

As the title of this chapter suggests, my intention is to discuss some selected aspects of economic policy-making in Singapore which I regard as particularly significant, without seeking to provide a comprehensive discussion of the evolution of policy over the past three decades or so. Specifically, the chapter will be organized around the themes of growthmanship, domestic demand, concern for others and social cohesiveness and the importance of passion.

GROWTHMANSHIP

Emphasis on high rates of GDP growth has been a hallmark of economic policy in Singapore since Independence.[40] Such growth can be

---

[40] See Chapter 2 for more on Singapore's GDP 'fetishism'. The reliance on foreign labour and its implications for equity are also discussed in Chapters 5 and 11.

achieved through a variety of positive means: capital accumulation, technological and skills upgrading, efficiency improvements, and the like. The import of professional and skilled foreign talent at a reasonable pace is also beneficial, it augments the economy's talent pool and reduces skill-scarcity-induced salary differentials.

However, Singapore has also relied on large imports of unskilled and lower-skilled foreign labour in its pursuit of GDP growth, and here the consequences are much more mixed. Such large inflows create a vicious circle: their availability reduces employers' incentives to upgrade their operations through further mechanization, automation and so on; the resulting low productivity levels imply that employers can only afford to offer low wages, which act as a disincentive to Singaporeans to take up such jobs; which in turn leads to continuing employer demands for inflows of foreign workers.

In a 1994 speech, Dr Lee Boon Yang, then Minister for Defence and Minister for Labour, quoted illustratively from a 1989 Construction Industry Development Board study:

> "In Perth, the cost of the two major construction inputs are considerably higher than those in Singapore. The prices of basic building materials are, on the average, 60% higher than Singapore's and all-in labour wages are 400% to 500% those in Singapore. However, the unit construction cost for luxury apartments, offices and hotels in Perth are only between five per cent and 11% higher than the corresponding levels reported for Singapore."[41]

More recent examples can also be given, such as the South Korean shipbuilding industry. A Wikipedia report, based in part on a *New York Times* article, observes:

> "The global shipbuilding industry is currently dominated by South Korea which is by far the world's largest shipbuilding nation. *In spite of high labour costs,* South Korea produced more ships in 2008 than the entire rest of the world's combined output. *Its preeminence in the industry is largely due to South Korea's highly advanced shipbuilding technology, the strong work ethic of*

---

[41] Speech at the annual dinner of the Singapore Contractors' Association Limited on December 1, 1994.

the labor force and the high productivity and efficiency of South Korean ship-yards. For example, the world's largest shipyard in Ulsan, operated by Hyundai Heavy Industries slips a newly-built, 80 million dollar vessel into the water every four working days."[42]

The time horizon is also important: there is a need for gradual but sustained adjustments in our foreign worker policy, which should have commenced earlier, but anyway can commence now. The intention should be not to eliminate the low-skilled foreign labour inflow altogether, but to tighten it over time, for example through levy increases. Recent policy pronouncements on this issue are in my view a step in the correct direction. To ease the burden of adjustment on businesses, consideration should be given to *announcing* a schedule of levy increases in advance (say by about six months prior to the first increase), so that businesses have time to start putting in place the necessary productivity-enhancing measures.

Consider also the following observation by Lim and Lee (2009), two keen observers of the Singapore scene:

> "The fact that government officials are rewarded economically, through salaries and bonuses, ... for delivering GDP growth, may also lead to 'growth fetishism'...and thus to preference for the easiest route to growth, which is through the addition of inputs of foreign capital, labour and skills."

This suggests that, as I have argued in more detail in a *Straits Times* article (Kapur, 2009), the GDP Bonus Scheme for civil servants should be modified. Consideration should be given to replacing it by a composite criterion comprising GDP growth, a broad-based measure of productivity growth of Singaporeans, such as the growth rate of *per capita* indigenous GDP, and a measure of the well-being of lower-paid Singaporeans. The latter might be proxied, for example, by the growth rate of the average household disposable income of the lowest 20% of Singaporeans. A composite criterion along these lines would serve to highlight more clearly some key priorities in policy-making.

---

[42] Wikipedia, 'Shipbuilding' (http://en.wikipedia.org/wiki/Shipbuilding), emphases added.

DOMESTIC DEMAND ISSUES

In 2008, Professor Linda Lim (2008) observed that 'it turns out that both China and Singapore have the world's lowest shares of consumption in GDP — about 40%'. GDP may not be the best 'deflator' for Singapore when studying Consumption at a point in time, owing to the high profits component in GDP, much accruing to foreign multinational companies. However, the trend over time is certainly indicative. From 1986–1987 to 1998–1999, the Consumption/GDP (C/GDP) ratio in Singapore went down from about 0.46 to 0.39, even as the wage share of GDP remained fairly constant, at around 0.42.

While low domestic demand has become an issue of policy concern in China, the same has not occurred in Singapore. One reason that has been advanced to explain why this need not be a significant policy concern is that in recent years domestic consumption growth contributed only a small fraction to overall GDP growth. However, this does not imply that the former could not contribute more to the latter if the C/GDP ratio were higher. Another reason that has been advanced is that meeting domestic demand is mainly useful if the local firms that cater to such demand eventually branch out into exports, thus increasing Singapore's earnings from the rest of the world.

But meeting domestic demands is also an economically valuable activity in its own right. Singapore residents derive benefits from consuming an entire array of tradable and nontradable items from more to less sophisticated ones — services of doctors, restaurants and hawker centres, barbers etc. Domestic production cannot obviously meet all our needs, so trade is necessary, but such production is still valuable. In a market economy, price generally reflects value to consumers closely. If one wishes to adopt a 'quasi-mercantilist' viewpoint, which is not necessary in my view, one could still argue that spending on nontradables diverts spending from tradables, helping to improve our trade balance. From a growth standpoint, small and medium sized enterprises often cater first to the local market, and, after acquiring experience, expand overseas. Examples are BreadTalk, Sakae Sushi, Charles & Keith, and OSIM.

At around 40%, Singapore's C/GDP ratio is far below that of another small economy, Hong Kong, which is over 60%. If we could move closer to the Hong Kong figure there would likely be larger scope for domestic enterprises to start up, grow, and expand into a wider range of markets. In some respects, therefore, production for the home market and for exports are complements. Moreover, as firms grow, they also tend to spend more on research and development, leading to new and better products and lower production costs.

Economists Tilak Abeysinghe and Choy Keen Meng have pointed out (Abeysinghe and Choy, 2007) that a significant factor behind the declining C/GDP ratio has been rising housing prices over the years. There could also be 'knock-on' effects: high private property prices tend to induce high Housing Development Board (HDB) resale prices, which in turn tend to raise the prices of new HDB flats given that, as the HDB indicated in 2007, the prices of new flats are based on the market prices of resale HDB flats, not on construction costs.[43]

The Ministry of National Development should, in my view, adopt measures such as increasing the rate of release of land sites to significantly moderate housing price increases, which will help to raise our C/GDP ratio over time. It might also have other benefits: for example, by reducing the pressure on married women to work full-time so as to afford increasingly expensive housing, it might well help to boost our fertility rate.[44] The need to monitor housing price increases takes on added importance when cognizance is taken of the targeted increase in Singapore's population to over 5 million.

CONCERN FOR OTHERS, SOCIAL COHESIVENESS

Arguably, we also wish to become a society characterized by concern for others, and social cohesiveness — a 'gracious society', in the true

---

[43] See Yap (2008).

[44] In fact, fertility-rate considerations might also justify a re-look at HDB flat affordability. If a young married couple decide that the wife should stay at home for about the first 7-8 years of marriage to bring up two young children, what size of flat could they typically afford bearing in mind that only one adult household member will be working during that period?

sense of the term. In addition to its intrinsic social worth, a more humane society commands greater loyalty and support from its citizens and encourages them to sink roots here. Two important issues in this respect are healthcare and distribution.

Healthcare Issues[45]

It is encouraging that the Ministry of Health (MOH) is now considering extending the Medishield coverage age beyond 80. In one area, however — subsidies for ARV-medication for HIV/AIDS victims — we come up glaringly short. In the *Straits Times* on December 1, 2008, Salma Khalik, Health Correspondent, wrote:

> "And unlike other major illnesses where there is at least one, sometimes as many as a dozen, medicines available to the poor at highly subsidized prices, there is no Government subsidy at all for the treatment of HIV here... Today, HIV is about the only major illness where patients do not enjoy any subsidies on medication."

Then in an article on December 6 she provided some good news:

> "People with HIV, who have long complained about the cost of medication here, are about to get some relief, the Government has decided to subsidise their medicines... Health Minister Khaw Boon Wan told *The Straits Times* he agreed with the view that HIV should be treated like any chronic disease...The committee of experts will apply the same approach as they do when evaluating drugs for other diseases. We should not single out HIV for special treatment."

Unfortunately, since the announcement was made, no further action was taken (as of October 2009 when this chapter was written). A couple of individuals raised the issue in the press in November 2009 and January 2010, and on January 16 *Today* reported: "It has taken a long time, but starting February 1, needy Singaporeans who

---

[45] The problem of healthcare financing for the elderly in Singapore is also taken up in Chapters 7 and 11.

require HIV treatments can turn to Medifund for assistance... Patients will be subject to means-testing, said MOH. It will inject S$8.5 million into Medifund, to be used for all needy Singaporean patients". It is to be hoped that all needy HIV cases will be adequately served by this arrangement.

Distributional Issues

I turn next to another set of issues, inspired by recent observations by Professor Tommy Koh (2009a, 2009b) in two recent *Straits Times* articles:

> "Unfortunately, that 'greed is good' culture [of Wall Street] has infected some Asian countries. Excessive pay for senior management, for example, has become fashionable in certain parts of Asia. This is not consistent with our communitarian values or our emphasis on team work and equity."

> "We seem to calculate everything in terms of money. We think that a person's worth is measured by the amount of money he or she makes. We have imitated one of the worst aspects of American capitalism, by paying our senior executives inflated salaries while, at the same time, stagnating the salaries of our middle and lower strata. As a result, Singapore has become a more unequal society than the United States."

In their book, *The Winner-Take-All Society*, economists Frank and Cook (1995) argue that very high salaries at the top in various occupations — such as management, banking and finance, movie-acting, and law — are largely due to (a) the widening of markets, owing to technological advances that lower communications, transport and other costs, and (b) heightened competition for top performers' salaries. Changing social norms also play a role.

They also argue that owing to negative externalities — each entrant into such competitions does not internalize the effect of his entry on others' prospects of winning — entry into such occupations tends to be socially excessive and at the expense of entry into other lesser-paid, but also socially valuable, occupations such as engineering, the sciences, and others.

A progressive income or expenditure tax system is thus in their view potentially efficiency-enhancing (and not only equity-enhancing), in discouraging excess entry into such occupations. They observe:

> "In Japan and Germany, for example, CEOs earn much lower salaries and face much higher tax rates than do their American counterparts... And yet the companies they manage have provided much of America's stiffest competition in recent years."

Some policies that Singapore might consider, in the light of the foregoing considerations, include an increase in the progressivity of our tax system, which currently is lower than the United States, and heightened incentives for students to pursue engineering and science degrees, such as through tuition subsidies (as also proposed by Frank and Cook).

THE IMPORTANCE OF PASSION

During his visit to Singapore in 1999, Nobel-Prize-winning physicist Steven Chu pointed out that true excellence in research cannot be motivated by material incentives: there has to be an intrinsic passion for it. In the area of business, Professor Charles Handy was quoted in *The Straits Times* of March 17, 1999 as saying:

> "Entrepreneurs have got to be passionate and totally committed to what they are doing. Now, I don't mean passionate and committed to making money, because that's just an outcome, but to what they're doing — whether they're crafting something beautiful, or making cameras, or starting an Internet business, or whatever."

An excellent academic rationale for the importance of passion may be found in Frank (1988), especially Chapter 4. Essentially, Frank adduces findings from experimental psychology to show that people generally have an innate pre-disposition towards 'short-termism', or 'time-inconsistent behaviour' so preferring immediate to delayed gratification in very near-term choices, even though they prefer the reverse when the same choices are presented to them at more distant horizons. People who are mainly concerned about material gain are thus likely to make ill-advised short-term choices which, ironically, reduce the material gain from their pursuits and activities, while those who have an intrinsic passion for the activities they engage in are likely to 'seek perfection' as best they can and, hence, end up being more successful. To do well materially, one should not be overly concerned about doing well materially.

What about the situation in Singapore? One writer, Phillip Holden (2006), has referred to the Singapore's developmental state's focus on material prosperity, or 'moneytheism' — a description which appears largely apt even today.[46] In characterizing the 'special and unique Lee Kuan Yew model of governance for Singapore', writer Catherine Lim has written in her blog, 'Its goal — total economic success', and she also makes reference to 'a culture so deeply attached to material wealth'.

Higher goals such as self-actualization, self-realization, and seeking to attain one's fullest creative potential, have not figured high in our system's priorities, at least not until recently, when the economic benefits of creativity began to be more widely appreciated!

In keeping with our materialistic motivations, our approach to social and economic engineering is largely of the 'carrot-and-stick' variety — which reinforces our materialism. One might well ask whether passion, creativity, imagination, the desire to excel for its own sake, and to help others excel, really flourish in such an environment.

For example, given our carrot-and-stick approach even to helping others to excel, is it any wonder that school-teachers and principals have in the past been motivated by examination-rankings-based performance criteria, with the severe effects it has had on the

---

[46] Holden is summarizing here the view of the late S. Rajaratnam, one of post-Independence Singapore's major political figures.

education of our children? Consider journalist Andy Ho's (2008) column of June 12, 2008:

> "There is an outcry about punitively difficult 'sure fail' exams that teachers set for students prior to the national PSLE, O levels and A levels...Is there not something dishonest in doing so? After all, national exams are not pitched at the same levels of difficulty...The authentic teacher...would not ever be a party to, or even consider setting, 'sure fail' exams. Exploitative tactics like these signal inauthenticity in the system. What teachers need to be first and foremost is to be real."

The foregoing discussion leads naturally to the most important question of all — how can passion be nurtured and fostered? May I be permitted to offer some tentative thoughts here. In my view, 'culture' in a broad sense, inclusive of religion and spirituality, has a key role to play — it sensitizes man to the nonmaterial dimensions of human existence, thus rendering him authentically human. 'Man does not live by bread alone'. Consideration should, I believe, be given to the introduction of courses on 'Comparative Cultures' in schools. Highlighting the commonalities across the world's great cultures — while recognizing that differences remain — will foster tolerance, greater understanding, and non-exclusivism.

It will also develop students' awareness and appreciation of the aesthetic and other non-material dimensions of the human experience, which could then foster their interests in other fields as well for their own sake — in other words, stimulate their passion.

Those who are metaphysically inclined might wish to note the following eloquent observation, which various spiritual traditions subscribe to: "The beauty that can be seen in all of creation is merely a reflection of God's artistic mastery".[47] This sense of beauty — which can be in art, physics, economics, engineering, etc. — is an enduring source of inspiration and passion. Ironically, effort in any field motivated by an enduring passion could well lead to more durable, sustained, material achievements, as Frank has argued, even though this cannot be the proximate motivation.

---

[47] This quote is from Sit (1998).

END NOTES

Abeysinghe, T and K M Choy (2007). *The Singapore Economy: An Econometric Perspective*. London: Routledge.

Frank, R (1988). *Passions within Reason: The Strategic Role of the Emotions*. New York: Norton.

Frank, R and P Cook (1995). *The Winner-Take-All Society*. New York: Free Press.

Ho, A (2008). No 'sure fail' exams with authenticity in teaching. *Straits Times*, June 12.

Holden, P (2006). Rajaratnam's tiger: Race, gender and the beginnings of Singapore nationalism. *Journal of Commonwealth Literature*.

Kapur, B (2009). Just a Numbers Game? Quality Counts Too. *Straits Times*, 15 September.

Koh, T (2009a). Learning from Two Crises. *Straits Times*, March 4.

Koh, T (2009b). Geneva of the East, Venice of 21st Century. *Straits Times*, August 19.

Lim, L (2008). Singapore's economic growth model — Too much or too little? Presented at the *Singapore Economic Policy Conference 2008*, Singapore Center for Applied Policy Economics, Department of Economics, National University of Singapore, October 24.

Lim, L and S A Lee (2009). Globalizing state, disappearing nation: Foreign participation in Singapore's economy. In Chong, T (ed.), *The Management of Success Revisited*, Singapore: Institute for Southeast Asian Studies.

Sit, M C (1998). *Christianity and Economics: A Selective Review of the Literature*. Unpublished Economics Academic Exercise, National University of Singapore.

Yap, E (2008). HDB pricing policy limits impact of rising costs. Singapore: *Business Times*, June 13.

REFORM OF THE INTERNATIONAL FINANCIAL ARCHITECTURE, THE G20 AND ASIA

Pradumna R Rana

INTRODUCTION

The Asian financial crisis of 1997–1998 had led to calls for the reform of the international financial architecture (IFA) or policies and practices of institutions that promote global financial stability. The crisis was triggered primarily by capital account factors associated with financial globalization, such as large inflows of foreign private capital and their sudden reversals, as opposed to current account problems.[48]

---

[48] Kawai (2010) notes that there were at least ten capital account crises in the 1990s: Mexico (February 1995), Argentina (April 1995; March 2000–January 2003), Thailand (August 1997), Indonesia (November 1997), Korea (December 1997), Russia (August 1998), Brazil (December 1998), Turkey (December 1999–February 2002), and Uruguay (2002).

It was felt that the International Monetary Fund (IMF) might not have adequate resources, especially compared with the scale of cross-border capital flows. It was also felt that several of the policy recommendations made by the IMF in managing the Asian financial crisis were not appropriate. With the V-shaped recovery from the crisis, complacency had set in and the reform measures were quickly forgotten (see Kawai and Rana, 2009, for a review of these issues). This partially set the stage for the present global crisis. At the global level, several institutions continued to recommend financial deregulation and capital account liberalisation even though they were recognized as having contributed to the crisis (United Nations, 2009). Moreover, many surplus countries started to individually accumulate international reserves to 'self-insure' themselves and this led to the widening of global imbalances that contributed to the present economic crisis.

The inadequacies of the responses of international financial institutions to the on-going financial crisis and their failure to take effective action to prevent it, has once again ignited interest in reforms to the IFA. It is argued that global finance is so interlinked that the current IFA is outdated. The Group of Twenty or G20 process for finance ministers and central bank governors, which was established in the aftermath of the Asian financial crisis, has been upgraded to the summit level or Leaders Process to spearhead, among others things, issues related to the IFA reforms. So far, three G20 Summits have been held: in Washington DC in November 2008, in London in April 2009, and in Pittsburgh in September 2009. There are, however, concerns that faster-than-expected recovery from the on-going crisis could lead to complacency on the reform of the IFA once again. If so, a big opportunity to reform the system will have been missed and, as before, vulnerabilities of countries to future crises will remain.

The objectives of this chapter are twofold: to outline the reforms that had been implemented during the post-Asian financial crisis period, including those that are now being implemented and considered under the auspices of the G20; and then to present several thoughts on the G20 process and how Asia can further strengthen its participation at this forum and be heard on issues related to global economic reforms.[49]

POST-ASIAN FINANCIAL CRISIS REFORMS OF THE INTERNATIONAL FINANCIAL ARCHITECTURE

Reform of the IFA in the aftermath of the Asian financial crisis was spearheaded by the Group of Eight or G8, while those in the aftermath of the present crisis have been spearheaded by the G20. Various organisations, such as the IMF, the World Bank and the Bank for International Settlements (BIS) have also played key supportive roles. These efforts are focused in the three areas of crisis prevention, crisis management/resolution, and IMF governance reforms.

Crisis Prevention

Standards and codes refer to provisions relating to the institutional environment or 'rules of the game' within which economic and financial policies are devised and implemented. The development, dissemination and adoption by countries of international standards are expected to assist countries in strengthening their economic institutions, inform market participants to allow for more effective market discipline and avoid herding behaviour, and provide inputs for IMF surveillance and World Bank country assistance strategies.

The IMF, World Bank, Organisation for Economic Cooperation and Development (OECD), International Organization of Securities Commissions IOSCO and BIS have established international standards in twelve areas, which are broadly categorised into three groups: policy transparency, financial sector regulation and supervision and market integrity. Standards in policy transparency include data transparency, fiscal transparency and monetary and financial

---

[49] The three steps recommended for Asia below will also be applicable for other regional groupings in Asia and Africa which participate in the G20 Summit.

policy transparency. Standards on financial sector regulation and supervision cover five areas: banking supervision, securities, insurance, payments systems, and anti-money laundering and combating the financing of terrorism. Standards of market integrity include corporate governance, accounting, auditing, and insolvency and creditor rights. A number of these standards are now being revised because they turned out to be 'pro-cyclical'. For example, several provisions in the Basel II framework encouraged banks to decrease the amount of capital they hold during business cycle expansions and increase them during contractions.

Data-dissemination standards help to enhance the availability of timely and comprehensive statistics and transparency, which in turn contribute to designing sound macroeconomic policies and taking sound policy action. The IMF has taken a number of steps to enhance information transparency and openness, including the establishment and strengthening of data-dissemination standards to help countries prevent future crises and diminish the effect of unavoidable ones.

The standards for data dissemination consist of two tiers. The first tier, called the Special Data Dissemination Standard (SDDS), was established in 1996 to guide countries that have, or might seek, access to international capital markets. The second tier, the General Data Dissemination System (GDDS), was established in 1997 to help countries provide more reliable data. The GDDS is focused on improving statistical systems, while the SDDS focuses on commitments to data dissemination standards in countries that already meet high data quality standards. Both are voluntary. Countries must also agree to post information about their data dissemination practices on the IMF's external website on the Dissemination Standards Bulletin Board (DSBB), and establish an Internet site containing the actual data, called a National Summary Data Page, to which the DSBB is linked.

It is also realised that problems in the financial system can reduce the effectiveness of monetary policy, create large fiscal costs related to bailing out troubled financial institutions, trigger capital flight and deepen economic recessions. Financial weaknesses in one country can also trigger contagion effects on others. A sound financial system is thus essential for supporting economic growth. This includes banks, securities exchanges, pension funds, insurers, the central bank and national regulators.

The IMF has sought to strengthen its surveillance. Surveillance refers to the process of regular dialogue and policy advice provided to member countries. It covers macroeconomic and financial developments and policies. Under the new Mid-term Strategy endorsed in September 2005, the IMF conducts multilateral consultations on common economic and financial issues with the first focusing on global payments imbalances. The first such surveillance involving several systemically important members, namely the United States, China, the Euro-zone, Japan and Saudi Arabia, was not very effective as the problem of global imbalances was serious in the pre-global economic crisis period and contributed to the crisis itself.

IMF surveillance is also fine-tuned to focus more systematically on regional developments, including increased dialogue with regional institutions and 'think tanks'. The IMF has also begun to publish regional outlook reports for the major regions of the world. IMF-supported programmes now include measures to strengthen financial systems, including financial assistance and assisting member countries to identify and diagnose financial system problems, designing strategies for systemic reforms and bank restructuring, and ensuring that these strategies are consistent with appropriate macroeconomic and structural policies.

A joint IMF-World Bank initiative, called the Financial Sector Assessment Programme (FSAP), was launched in 1999. This provides member countries with a comprehensive evaluation of their financial systems, with a view to alerting national authorities about vulnerabilities in their financial sectors and assisting them in designing measures to reduce weaknesses. The FSAP also determines the development needs of the financial sector. Sectoral developments and risks and vulnerabilities are analysed using a range of financial soundness indicators and macro-financial stress tests. Other areas of financial stability are also analysed, including systemic liquidity arrangements, institutional frameworks for crisis management and loan recovery, transparency, accountability and governance. The IMF had reportedly

requested the United States to undergo an FSAP prior to the outbreak of the sub-prime mortgage crisis, but it was only at the end of
2007 that the United States agreed to do so. After the outbreak of
the crisis, the Financial Stability Forum (FSF) was upgraded to the
Financial Stability Board (FSB) with a bigger mandate and a larger
membership. All G20 countries have now been included and the total
membership is 25.

Financial crises in emerging market economies have demon-
strated that abrupt or improperly sequenced liberalisation of the
balance of payments capital account can generate vulnerabilities and a
crisis. A sudden surge in capital inflows and a sudden stop or reversal
of capital flows can precipitate a crisis. This is an important lesson
learnt from the Asian financial crisis. The most important thing to do
is to establish a core institutional infrastructure in the form of well-
defined property and creditor rights, credible accounting standards,
benchmark corporate governance, clear minority rights and stringent
prudential and regulatory regimes. However, the IMF continues to
promote financial, including capital market liberalization, although
the Articles of Agreement clearly allow governments to use capital
controls (UN, 2009). The need for a sequenced deregulation of the
capital account is an important lesson learnt from the present crisis.
Recently, Brazil introduced a 2% tax on foreign purchases of equity
and debt. Other countries are also considering similar measures.
There are now tentative signs that the IMF is supportive of temporary controls on capital flows.

At the Pittsburgh G20 Summit, the Leaders agreed to initiate a
peer review process or "a cooperative process of mutual assessment of
policy frameworks and the implications of those frameworks for the
pattern and sustainability of global growth" to try to prevent a financial crisis. They went on to add that "G20 members will set out
medium-term policy frameworks and will work together to assess the
collective implications of national policy frameworks for the level and
pattern of global growth and identify potential risks to financial stability". The IMF is to help "with its analysis of how respective
national and regional policy frameworks fit together". The World
Bank is to advise on progress in promoting development and poverty

reduction. The FSB is to monitor progress in implementing regulatory and supervisory reforms and, together with the IMF, is to undertake 'macro-prudential' monitoring to provide early warnings of systemic risks.

On strengthening the financial regulatory system, there appears to have been a broad agreement on the need for tightening regulations, both at the national and international level. However, partly reflecting the complexity of the issues, views differ on how best to regulate and the degree of regulation. The G20 Leaders have pledged to develop internationally agreed rules to improve the quantity and quality of bank capital by the end of 2010 and implement them by 2012. All standardised over-the-counter derivatives contracts are to be traded on electronic trading platforms, where appropriate, and cleared through central clearinghouses by the end of 2012. They also endorsed guidelines for bankers' pay but indicated that the FSB is to propose additional measures by March 2010. International accounting bodies are to develop a single set of new global accounting standards by June 2011.

Crisis Management

In order to play its role in safeguarding international financial stability, in the immediate aftermath of the Asian financial crisis in November 1998, the IMF established a New Arrangements to Borrow (NAB), thereby doubling its resources. Further increases were made in response to the current crisis. The second G20 Summit in London in April 2009 had pledged to provide more resources (US$1.1 trillion) to the IMF and other multilateral institutions. In Pittsburgh, the G20 Leaders announced that they had delivered on this promise. The G20 has committed over US$500 billion to a renewed and expanded NAB and the IMF has made a new Special Drawing Right allocation of US$283 billion. However, the latter was allocated among IMF members in line with existing quotas, which means that the G8 members, which do not need liquidity support from the IMF, actually received a large chunk of it (45%).

The Contingent Credit Line (CCL) was introduced in 1999 as part of the IMF's efforts to strengthen member countries' defences against financial crises. The CCL is intended to be a precautionary line of defence to help protect countries pursuing relatively robust policies in the event of a liquidity need arising from the spread of financial crises. For various reasons, however, the facility was never used and in November 2003 it was allowed to expire.

In 2008, the IMF reintroduced a CCL in the form of a new Short-term Liquidity Facility (SLF) to offer quick large-scale financing without specific conditionality. But even the SLF proved inadequate. In March 2009 it was replaced by a Flexible Credit Line (FCL) which provides pre-qualified countries with large amounts of resources without *ex-post* conditions to manage financial contagion. The FCL also allows a longer repayment period of 31/4 to five years. Three countries: Colombia, Mexico and Poland have been provided credits totalling US$78 billion under this facility.

At the time of the Asian financial crisis the IMF came in for harsh criticism for prescribing too many structural reforms. For example, the Indonesian programme had over 100 conditions including the dismantling of the clove monopoly. Over time, the IMF has streamlined its programmes to limit structural conditionality to a core set of essential features that are macro-relevant and in the IMF's core area of responsibility,[50] with a broader approach requiring justification based upon the specific country's situation. More recent IMF-supported programmes appear to have been tailored to the individual country's circumstances. To some extent, the IMF now seems ready to move away from its 'one-size-fits-all' approach to stabilisation. Recent programmes for Iceland, Costa Rica, Hungary, Guatemala, Serbia and Latvia allow for fiscal stimulus and deficits, and exchange rate stabilization. But how widely this flexibility will be used remains to be seen.

---

[50] The IMF's core areas of responsibility include macroeconomic stabilization; monetary, fiscal and exchange rate policy, including the underlying institutional arrangements and closely related structural measures, and financial sector issues, including the functioning of both domestic and international financial markets.

In the post-Asian financial crisis period, the international community started to explore possible mechanisms for official standstill provisions or private sector involvement. It focused on the debt restructuring of international sovereign bonds with the recognition that, at the time of a liquidity crisis, holders of sovereign bonds, along with other creditors, would need to contribute to the resolution of such crises. Two methods were recommended: a contractual approach and a statutory approach. A contractual approach considers collective action clauses (CACs) in sovereign bond contracts as a device for orderly resolution of crises; their explicit inclusion in bond documentation would provide a degree of predictability to the restructuring process. A statutory approach, such as the Sovereign Debt Restructuring Mechanism, attempts to create the legal basis through a universal treaty rather than through a set of national laws in a limited number of jurisdictions, for establishing adequate incentives for debtors and creditors to agree upon a prompt, orderly and predictable restructuring of unsustainable debt. The CACs approach was subsequently adopted while a more comprehensive statutory approach was put on hold. However, the lack of a sovereign debt restructuring mechanism, a *de facto* international bankruptcy procedure, continues to make crisis resolution difficult as recently in Iceland and the Baltic states.

Reform of the IMF Governance

These reforms refer to quotas and voting rights, executive board representation and the management of the IMF. The IMF quotas and voting rights must be substantially realigned to better recognise the economic and financial weight of emerging markets, including those in Asia. Presently, the industrial countries as a group hold about 60% of the quotas and voting rights with the emerging markets holding 20% and the rest of the developing countries holding the remaining 20%. These ratios have not changed significantly over time and do not reflect the growing size of emerging markets in the global economy. Since 85% of the votes are required for decision-making, the United States, which holds 17% of the quota, is the only country that has a veto at the IMF.

At the 2006 annual meeting of the IMF and the World Bank held in Singapore, a decision was taken to increase the quotas of China, Mexico, Korea and Turkey by small amounts. In April 2008, an agreement was reached to increase quotas of a larger number of countries (54) by also a small amount. But this agreement has yet to be implemented. Quota reform is a highly charged issue as it means a loss of power for countries that have a strong voice at the IMF. At the Pittsburgh Summit, the Leaders pledged to transfer at least 5% of the squota to emerging markets by January 2011. Occupying eight of the 24 chairs and represented in another constituency at the IMF Board, there is a feeling that European countries are over-represented at the IMF. With the establishment of a monetary union, Europe should occupy fewer seats. However, aside from the broad statements made, little concrete action has been taken so far.

Finally, as Mahbubani (2008) has pointed out, the rule that the head of the IMF should be a Western European automatically dis-qualifies 88% of the world's population from leadership of this global economic institution. As he and many others have argued, the choice of the IMF head should be based on merit and qualifications and not on nationality. This issue has also not been addressed as yet.

The slow progress in reforming the IMF continues to be a problem. This was the case in the aftermath of the Asian financial crisis when many felt that the IMF had lost legitimacy in its operations and was sidelined. Its lending operations had declined significantly and it was also suffering from a precarious financial situation. The IMF credit out-standing, which had peaked at almost US$100 billion at the end of 2005, had declined to about US$10 billion by the end of September 2008. The IMF's income, which is related to its lending operations, had dwindled and staff retrenchments had begun. In the aftermath of the present crisis, questions related to legitimacy and effectiveness continue to be raised as little progress has been made in reforming its governance.

THE G20 AND ASIA

As outlined above, while some progress has been made in the areas of crisis prevention and crisis management, progress in reforming the

IMF governance has been limited. Can the faster-than-expected recovery from the crisis that we are now witnessing all over the world once again lead to complacency and postponement of reforms? Probably not this time around. This is because the present round of reforms is being overseen by the G20 in which systemically important developing countries, who are stakeholders, have a voice. In contrast, earlier efforts were under the auspices of the G8 where only the industrial countries were included.

Although it is still too early to judge, there are two ways of looking at the achievements of the G20 Summits so far. A clear winner has been the IMF. As mentioned above, in the immediate pre-crisis period the IMF was perceived by many as an institution that had lost legitimacy and was heading towards irrelevance, mainly due to its mismanagement of the Asian crisis. The on-going current crisis has elevated the IMF to an innovative crisis-responder. Its lending volume, which had dwindled to US$10 billion in 2007, has increased to US$160 billion (the peak was US$150 billion in 2005). The recent request by the European Union to the IMF to take part in the rescue of Greece has also enhanced its clout. The IMF's lending capacity has also been tripled to US$750 billion by the G20, which has also given it, together with the FBS, an important role in its newly established 'peer review process'.

To its credit, the IMF under Dominique Strauss-Kahn, who took over in late 2007, has re-invented itself to a large extent by streamlining conditionality and by introducing new credit lines. This turnaround is to be applauded. Nevertheless, the institution continues to lack legitimacy and the trust of many members and continues to be viewed as an agent of western countries. When Korea faced financing difficulties in 2009 it went to the US Federal Reserve rather than the IMF. One Korean finance official was reported to have said, "South Koreans tremble and financial markets turn sensitive whenever they hear the word 'IMF'". Furthermore, as Subramanian (2010) warned, "The IMF remains more lenient to Europeans than others and risks being labelled a 'Euro-Atlantic Monetary Fund'". Several Eastern European countries, including Hungary, Romania and Ukraine have large IMF programmes.

The lack of legitimacy stems from the limited progress made in reforming its governance as Western countries are reluctant to give up their political power at the IMF. Eventually, the G20 must put its money where its mouth is and place reform of the IMF governance at the top of its agenda, otherwise all its other achievements will lack effectiveness. If so, as noted by the Stiglitz Commission (United Nations, 2009), the future global architecture could comprise a network of regional monetary funds, such as the Asian Monetary Fund and the African Monetary Fund, working in coordination with a trimmer IMF.

A broader view is that the developing world has also come out as a winner. At the Pittsburgh Summit, the Leaders designated the G20 as the 'premier forum' for international economic cooperation replacing the G8, which is to focus more on security and foreign policy issues. At that Summit, President Obama announced that the G20 would replace the G8. As compared to the Western-dominated G8, the G20 brings the main industrialised countries together with systemically important developing countries, such as China, India and Brazil. This decision is historic because it recognises the growing economic weight of developing countries in the world economy and represents the passing of the baton to them. Notably, in his State of the Union address in January this year, and unlike in the past, President Obama did not mention the G8.

Another reason why the Pittsburgh Summit is historic is that it introduced a 'peer review' system of each member's macroeconomic and financial policies.[51] This is because in a globalised world policies spill over national boundaries. The IMF is to help the G20 assess collective implications and the potential risks of the sum of their disparate growth strategies. The World Bank is also to help in promoting

---

[51] This peer review process is historic because, apart from the Trade Policy Review Body of the World Trade Organization, where peer review of trade policies is conducted, there is no institution where representatives of both the industrial and the developing world sit across or around the table to conduct a peer review of macroeconomic or financial sector policies.

development and poverty reduction as part of the rebalancing of global growth. And the FBS and IMF are to help jointly in macro-prudential monitoring to help prevent credit and asset price cycles from becoming forces of destabilisation.

The G20 Summit should, however, be seen as a process and not as an event. The group is self-appointed and at this point in time it is difficult to see how it will evolve in the future. The first Summit was held in November 2008 and so far only three Summits have been held. Two more are slated for 2010, in Canada (June) and in Korea (November). One important issue facing the G20 is that of inclusiveness. The G20 represents 4.2 billion people of the world but not the other 2.6 billion. How can their views be incorporated and the legitimacy of the G20 be enhanced? While addressing this question, it must be borne in mind that there is a trade-off between effectiveness and inclusiveness. The more inclusive the group, the less effective it can be.

Three possible approaches can be considered. The first is for the left-out countries to form a coalition of the unrepresented, a group of their own. But even if they were successful in establishing such a coalition, it is not clear how the coalition could obtain a seat at the G20 table unless their representative is invited to the G20, as in the 3G proposal made by Singapore (discussed below).

The second is inclusiveness through the involvement of the United Nations. The Stiglitz Commission notes that decisions concerning necessary reforms to the IFA must not be made by a self-selected group, such as the G7, G8 or the G20, but by all countries of the world, working in concert. Better representation and democratic legitimacy will not require the presence of all countries in all deliberations. Working committees chosen by a democratic process can be limited to a size that ensures effective decision-making (United Nations, 2009). This proposal certainly merits further consideration, but the view that the UN lacks competencies to engage in matters of systemic reform, has to be overcome.

The third approach would be to continue the present G20 practice of inviting representatives of various regional groupings. Under the present system, regional organisations such as The Association of

Southeast Asian Nations (ASEAN), the Asia Pacific Economic Forum, the African Union Commission and the New Partnership for Africa's Development are invited to G20 Summits. Other representatives of regional groupings could also be invited as appropriate.

A related issue is that of the G20 agenda. So far the focus has been on the continuation of stimulus packages that bring about faster-than-expected recovery globally, coordination of exit strategies and the design of a new international financial regulatory framework. Issues of trade and IMF governance that are of relevance to developing countries have figured less prominently in the G20 discussions. For example, the Leaders' statement from the Pittsburgh Summit mentions, "We are determined to seek an ambitious and balanced conclusion to the Doha Development Round in 2010". But no concrete actions are mentioned as to how this important objective is to be achieved. Some have made the case for the G20 to address long-term issue, such as the reform of the United Nations and action on climate change. Despite the above issues, it is unlikely that the G20 will simply fade away any time soon.

THE WAY FORWARD FOR ASIA

Now that they have been invited to participate in the discussions, the onus is on developing countries to make sure that they are heard effectively at the G20. In particular, how can Asia leverage its growing economic weight into more effective participation in the G20? Asia is represented there by six countries: Australia, China, India, Indonesia, Korea and Japan. How can these countries further synergise and leverage their individual country's economic and political weight and come up with Asian perspectives for a more effective participation in the G20?

First, realising the centrality of ASEAN in the Asian regional architecture, Asian countries should lobby to formalise the membership of ASEAN representatives in the G20. Under the present G20 practice of inviting representatives of regional groupings, the ASEAN Chair and the ASEAN Secretary-General participated at the London and the Pittsburgh Summits. Asian countries should lobby to formalise and regularise the participation of the ASEAN Chair and the ASEAN Secretary-General in future G20 Summits.[52] In this context, the ASEAN Leaders' Statement from the Hanoi Summit of April 9, 2010 that "ASEAN strongly believes that it can contribute to the deliberations of the G20 through the continued participation of the ASEAN Chair and the ASEAN Secretary-General in the future G20 Summits"[53] is a step in the right direction.

Second, Asian countries should organise meetings of the expanded ASEAN+3, which adds South Korea, Japan and China to ASEAN, just prior to the G20 Summits to coordinate policies and develop common views and opinions to support the participation of the ASEAN representatives in the G20. After the Asian financial crisis, a number of fora have been established in the region for policy coordination. These include the Executives' Meeting of East Asian and Pacific Central Bankers and the ASEAN Surveillance Process, which brings together the 10 ASEAN finance ministers and their deputies. Although ASEAN plays the central role in the region's institutional architecture, it is the ASEAN+3 Economic Review and Policy Dialogue (ERPD) which brings together the finance ministers and deputies of the 13 ASEAN+3 that is much more comprehensive and has strong technical support, which is critically important.

Under the ASEAN+3 ERPD, Finance Ministers of the ASEAN+3 countries meet once a year and their deputies twice a year for two days at a time to assess global, regional, and national conditions and risks; review financial sector (including bond market) developments and vulnerabilities and discuss other topics of mutual interest. These issues are then elevated to the Finance Ministers' meeting.

The ASEAN+3 ERPD has been strengthened significantly to support the Chiang Mai Initiative Multilateralization (CMIM).[54] For

---

[52] As discussed later in the chapter, the G3 also supports this idea.

[53] ASEAN Leaders' Statement on Sustained Recovery and Development, Hanoi, 9 April 2010.

[54] CMIM refers to the US$120 billion multilateral currency swap scheme or crisis fund launched by the ASEAN+3 in March 2010.

example, it has established a system to monitor financial sector vulnerability and an early warning system for banking and financial crises. In addition to the ASEAN+3 countries and their growing economic linkages with the region, India, Australia and New Zealand should also be invited to participate in these regional meetings. The deliberations of the 'expanded' ASEAN+3 prior to the G20 Summits will provide a robust agenda for the ASEAN representatives to table at the Summit.[55] The ASEAN representatives can contribute substantive ideas to the global body and participate effectively in these meetings.[56] Once the ASEAN+3 Macroeconomic Research Office (AMRO), an independent surveillance agency to support CMIM is established in Singapore by May 2011, the AMRO could convene the policy dialogue meetings of the 'expanded' ASEAN+3.[57]

Third, Asian countries should coordinate their views and positions with those of developing countries in other regions of the world by supporting and being members of the informal 3G. This group presently comprises about two dozen small and medium states, of which four are from Asia (Brunei, Malaysia, Philippines and Singapore), which have come together to develop a constructive dialogue on coordination and cooperation between G20 and non-G20 members. The 3G has been convened by Singapore under the auspices of the United Nations since July 2009.

The 3G has put forward a few ideas (Menon, 2010). First, the G20 should undertake consultations as widely as possible with non-G20 members before the G20 Summits. Second, the UN Secretary-General should be an active participant in all aspects of the

---

[55] Both the ASEAN Chair and the ASEAN Secretary-General participate in the ASEAN+3 ERPD.

[56] The East Asia Summit (EAS) group comprises the 16 countries under discussion, but it has so far focused on cultural and social issues and does not yet engage in economic policy coordination. The first informal East Asia Summit Finance Ministers' meeting was held in Tashkent, Uzbekistan in May 2010.

[57] For the decision to establish the AMRO, see the Joint Statement of the 14th ASEAN Finance Ministers' Meeting of April 8 2010, which is available at aseansecretariat.org.

G20 process. Third, the G20 process should take on a 'variable geometry' configuration to allow non-G20 states to participate in Ministerial and other gatherings and other working groups involving senior officials/experts on specialised issues. Fourth, the G20 should continue the practice of inviting established regional groupings to the Summits. In fact, the presence of regional groupings at the G20 meetings should be formalised. These ideas have been incorporated in a 3G paper entitled 'Strengthening the Framework for G20 Engagement with Non-members' and has been circulated as a United Nations document.

END NOTES

Kawai, M (2010). Reform of the international financial architecture: An Asian perspective. *Singapore Economic Review*, 1, 207–242.

Kawai, M and P B Rana (2009). The Asian financial crisis revisited: Lessons, responses and new challenges. In Carney, R (ed.), *Lessons from the Asian Financial Crisis*. New York: Routledge, pp. 155–197.

Mahbubani, K (2008). *The New Asian Hemisphere: The Irresistible Shift of Global Power to the East*. Public Affairs.

Menon, Vanu Gopal (2010). *Global Governance: The G20 and the UN*, available at www.ipsterraviva.net/UN/print.aspx?idnews+N7370.

Subramanian, A (2010). *IMF Crisis Balance Sheet*, available at www.iie.com/realtime/?p=942.

United Nations (2009). *Report of the Commission of Experts of the President of the UN General Assembly on Reforms of the International Monetary and Financial System*. New York: United Nations, September 12.

THE CURRENT PRODUCTIVITY DRIVE IN SINGAPORE AND LABOUR MARKET POLICIES

Chew Soon Beng and Rosalind Chew

INTRODUCTION

During the 2008–2009 financial crisis, it was observed that the West was experiencing a structural problem while Singapore and other Asian countries were experiencing a cyclical problem. Both the West and Asia adopted expansionary demand management policies to deal with their economic problems and boost domestic demand and/or protect jobs. An expected consequence of such an approach is that the former will incur rising public debt while the structural problem persists (Sheng, 2009).

As for Singapore and other Asian countries, their economies rebounded rather quickly but suffered from asset inflation. To a large extent, the Singapore economy did not do so badly in 2009 because of the adoption of various labour market policies to trim costs to save jobs; and the quick recovery of global demand. Singapore is now out of the recession although global recovery is still a little uncertain and the Singapore government has embarked on a national drive to increase productivity growth to 2% to 3% per year for the next ten years (Ministry of Finance, 2010).

The foundation of economic management in Singapore is sound because Singapore has been able to manage its labour market to achieve competitiveness. The purpose of this chapter is to ask whether labour market management principles have been changed or modified as a result of the global crisis and whether these principles have to change further to achieve Singapore's National Productivity Goal.

NATIONAL WAGES COUNCIL, WAGE SYSTEMS AND THE CENTRAL PROVIDENT FUND

Since self-government in 1959, Singapore has actively sought foreign investment as the main instrument to attain GDP growth.[58] The separation of Singapore from Malaysia in 1965 accelerated this need to attract foreign investment. Due to the pragmatic policies adopted, Singapore was so successful in attracting labour-intensive firms to Singapore that the country experienced a labour shortage in the late 1960s. To overcome this, Singapore encouraged married women to enter/return to the labour force and began to allow foreign workers to work in Singapore in large numbers (Lim and Associates, 1988). As wages started to show signs of rapid increase, the Singapore government set up the National Wages Council (NWC) in 1972 to allow wage growth in an orderly manner. The NWC, which is a tripartite body managed to change workers' perceptions by announcing non-mandatory wage increase guidelines from 1972 onwards (Lim and Chew, 1998).

In the following years from 1973 to 1987, the NWC only issued quantitative wage guidelines. However, since 1988, NWC has only

---

[58] For some more background on this policy, see Chapter 2.

issued *qualitative* wage guidelines. NWC has also been involved in non-wage issues such as wage reform, training, and age of retirement. We will discuss the role of the NWC in the post-global crisis period subsequently.

In the 1960s, the most prevalent wage system was the seniority-based system, under which workers' wages generally increased with the length of service. Of course, in Singapore, as in other Commonwealth countries, both employees and employers have to contribute to the respective employee's Central Provident Fund (CPF) account. The wage cost of employing a worker is thus their wages plus the amount contributed by his employer to the CPF account. The CPF has evolved into a social security scheme to achieve the long-term objectives of home ownership, retirement needs and medical expenses in a sustainable manner (Chew and Chew, 2008).

Singapore's industrial development progressed well (Lim and Associates, 1988). In 1978, when China declared that she was going to embark on economic reform, the NWC proposed that the island republic increase labour costs to get Singapore out of the low-wage trap. The main instrument used to achieve this was the employer's CPF contribution rate, which was raised from 16.5% in 1978 to 25% by the mid-1980s. The high labour cost policy achieved the purpose of industrial upgrading. Many labour-intensive firms left Singapore for Malaysia. GDP growth was good and productivity growth was 5% per year for the 1980s. The harmonious relationship among the workers, employers and the government was cemented during this period when wage guidelines were generally very high from the late 1970s to the early 1980s.

But the 1985 recession took Singapore by surprise. Singapore's exports were not competitive, and high labour costs were part of the problem. Consequently, the NWC proposed the reduction of the employer's CPF contribution rate from 25% to 10% in 1986 to save jobs. Due to the timeliness of the measure and the drastic cut in wage costs, the Singapore economy recovered in 1987.

It is obvious that, as the CPF is an instrument for achieving long-term social objectives and because it is also a blunt instrument, using the CPF scheme as a short-term macroeconomic policy tool is not advisable. During a cyclical downturn, wage costs should be reduced internally within the wage system. Consequently, the NWC began to promote the flexible wage system after 1988. Under this system, wage costs are downward flexible in a recession as bonuses will be smaller or even zero.

During the 1997 East Asian Currency crisis, the Singapore dollar depreciated against the US dollar by about 18%. As the flexible wage system was not widely implemented in Singapore at that time, and because the timing and quantum of bonus payments is not uniform, the NWC again proposed that the employer's CFP contribution rate be reduced from 20% to 10%. Because of the reluctance to continue to rely on the CPF scheme to reduce wage costs during a downturn, the NWC proposed the introduction of the Monthly Variable Component (MVC) as a special case of a flexible wage system. The MVC wage system has a monthly wage component that can be taken away either partially or wholly in a downturn.[59]

In the first half of 2008, inflation worldwide was high and the inflation rate in Singapore was 5%. The NWC proposed that employers grant a one-time lump sum payment to low-income workers to offset the erosion of purchasing power caused by high inflation.

Apart from the issue of wage flexibility, increasing life expectancy means that workers are expected to remain engaged in the labour force for a longer period of time. The NWC first proposed that the age of retirement be raised from 55 to 60 in the early 1990s. In 2000, the NWC again proposed that it be raised from 60 to 62, and in 2007 that it be raised to 65 by 2012. In late 2008, the Tripartite Taskforce also urged employers to reduce costs in other areas, emphasizing that retrenching workers should be the last resort. It surprised many that the NWC was silent on this matter.

On a quarter-to-quarter basis, the Singapore economy registered a revised negative GDP growth of 15.2% in the fourth quarter of 2008. Consequently, the government announced that it would use

---

[59] There were, however, some reservations on the part of the workers. See Chew and Chew (2008).

Singapore's past official foreign exchange reserves to help pay employers' CPF contributions through the Jobs Credit Scheme to save jobs, as well as to finance the absentee payroll of workers who attend sponsored training programmes (Ministry of Finance, 2009). Hence training is also targeted as a key measure aimed at saving jobs.

PRO-MARKET TRAINING SCHEMES

There is a market failure in training because employers generally do not want to invest in the training of their workers due to high turnover. The Skills Development Fund (SDF) was set up in 1979 to encourage employers to train their workers. The government overcomes such market failure by first imposing a SDF levy on employers. The SDF then uses these same funds to subsidize employers who choose the training programmes to train their workers on a co-payment basis (generally, employers have to pay 30% of the training cost). The number of SDF trainees has decreased from 575,000 in 1999 to 384,000 in 2007 although the per trainee grant has increased over the years. The decline in the number of SDF trainees is more than offset by those in the Singapore Workforce Development Agency (WDA). The WDA, which was set up in 2000, pays more attention to the training of SMEs, the unemployed and those workers who need to change employers. With the combined efforts of both the SDF and the WDA, one can safely say that, on the average, every worker of Singapore's 1.6 million workforce receives training once every four years. This is a great achievement. Nevertheless, the SDF and the WDA have to step up their efforts in order that the national productivity goal can be achieved and sustained.

During a recession, the SDF is reinforced by SPUR (Skills Programme for Upgrading and Resilience). SPUR, which is administrated by the WDA, pays 90% of the training costs and also 90% of the absentee payroll. SPUR is a key feature in the 2009 Budget to improve the skills of workers while their jobs are protected. SPUR will be phased out in 2010.

Both the SDF and the WDA reach out to workers whose employers can be motivated by the SDF to train their workers. However, causal workers and unskilled workers, especially those in the informal sector, generally fall through the nets of the SDF and the WDA. No-one should be left behind in economic development and Singapore aims to achieve such an outcome.

THE NO-ONE IS LEFT BEHIND STRATEGY[60]

School dropouts do not do well in any society (Borgas, 2010). Although there are not many pupils not completing either primary or secondary school in Singapore, the government has a web of vocational and training schemes to ensure that no-one is left behind due to lack of opportunities. The reason is obvious. Less enterprising youngsters face relentless competition from low-wage foreign workers in Singapore. If nothing is done to help them, they may become low-income working adults. Generally, their children will also end up not doing well academically and consequently become low-income workers as well. They will be caught in the poverty cycle and the productivity drive will be retarded.

On a year-to-year basis, there were 50,655 primary six students in 2006, but there were 50,687 secondary one students in 2007. The increase in the number of secondary one students over the number of primary six students indicates that attrition from the Singapore school system is minimal and that there is immigration.

There were, in 2006, 61,689 secondary four students (secondary five students from the Normal stream are also included here). About 28% (17,156) of these proceeded to junior colleges, 22% (13,834) to the Institute for Technical Education (ITE), and 39% (24,126) to polytechnics. This leaves about 11% of this cohort of secondary four students to account for. Hence, every year, there are about 6,000 to 7,000 youngsters in each secondary four cohort who do not proceed to further their education. It is possible that many in this group choose to work and study part-time at ITE, while others find

---

[60] This is part of a broader social contract between the government and its citizens as explained in Chapter 11.

employment in the informal sector. Government strategy is to ensure that ITE graduates can be gainfully employed and that young workers receive effective training.

Institute for Technical Education (ITE)

ITE admits only school-leavers who have completed secondary education. They can choose to take up a course either under full-time or traineeship modes of training. Full-time (ITE education) courses are conducted on a semester credit system which is more flexible. Depending on the course, full-time ITE students can generally obtain ITE certification within two to three years. Full-time programmes, which lead to the award of the Higher National ITE Certificate (Higher Nitec) and National ITE Certificate (Nitec), are offered in the areas of engineering and technical skills, business and services, information communications technology and applied and health sciences.

On an "earn as you learn" basis, traineeship courses run for one to three years depending on the level of training. Traineeship comprises two components: off-the-job and on-the-job training. In the off-the-job training component, trainees are taught technical concepts and knowledge. This training component may be conducted in an ITE campus, an industry training centre or on the company's premises. Under the on-the-job component, trainees apply the knowledge and concepts learnt during the off-the-job training. ITE's assessment comes in the form of trainees being assigned a supervisor who is trained to oversee their actual performance at work.

The government of Singapore pays particular attention to vocational education via ITE because it does not want to make the same mistake made by many countries in ignoring the education of youngsters who are not academically inclined. On a per student basis, in 2007, government expenditure on a primary school student and a secondary student was S$5,123 and S$7,234 respectively. Expenditure on each polytechnic and university student was S$12,510 and S$19,404 respectively. But for vocational education, which is often ignored by most countries, the government expenditure on each ITE student was S$10,343 which was about 83% of the expenditure on each polytechnic student (Chew and Chew, 2010b).

The starting mean monthly salary of ITE graduates ranged from S$1,163 to S$1,375 in 2007. This compares very well with the starting salary of polytechnic diploma holders of S$1,522 to S$2,300 and the starting salary of public university graduates of S$2,500 to S$3,700. There is opportunity for progression for ITE graduates who can proceed to a polytechnic and then to a university. The employment rate of fresh ITE graduates six months after taking their exams in 2007 ranged from 66% for Nitec certificate in Business and Technical to 94% for Nitec in Nursing (Chew and Chew, 2010b).

ITE graduates are likely to be working in occupations such as Services Workers and Clerical Workers. However, if they proceed to polytechnic education for further studies, and many of them do, they can move to a better occupation, such as Associate Professionals and Technicians, for which the salary is much higher.

Hence, in the continued effort to increase productivity nationwide, the role of ITE is paramount.

Training of Casual Workers

In Singapore, low-wage workers receive Workfare. In 2008, there were almost 290,000 Workfare recipients. Some of these did not complete primary, secondary, or vocational education. They are unskilled and casual workers. If Singapore is to attain 2% to 3% productivity growth per year, the skills of Workfare recipients must be raised via training. WTS (Workfare Training Scheme) will pay for 90% of training costs and 90% of absentee payroll but only for Workfare recipients (Ministry of Finance, 2010). WTS is similar to SPUR except that the latter is available only during recessions. WTS clearly shows that the government is determined to achieve inclusive growth.

ITE also offers six-month modules in Engineering, Info-Communications Technology, Business and Services for workers who have completed secondary education. Those who lack formal education qualifications are encouraged to attend other six-month modules to attain the necessary academic qualifications before taking on more formal ITE training programmes. These modules are known as Basic Education for Skills Training (BEST), Worker Improvement through Secondary Education (WISE) and Continuing Education.

Alternatively, some of this group may enroll in Employability and Skills (ESS) training programmes operated by the government. ESS is recognized by both the government and 300 companies in Singapore as an alternative to formal academic qualifications such as O-Levels. ESS offers training in Workplace Literacy Series, Workplace Numeracy Series and Workplace Skills Series. If they can follow this path persistently (Figure 1), they can be gainfully employed. However, not all of this group of young workers will have the endurance to complete the training. If they do not take any, or take only some of these programmes, it is likely that they will remain low-wage workers and will be the target of self-help bodies, such as the Chinese Assistance Development Council (CDAC).

The training of low-wage workers in Singapore is also the responsibility of the self-help bodies which are organized according to the

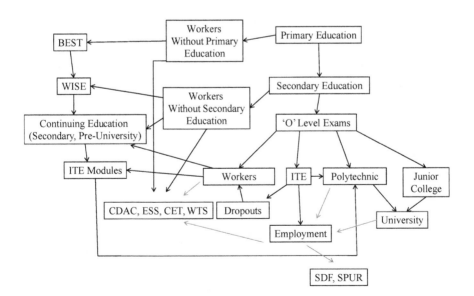

Figure 1: Singapore's Inclusive Training Schemes.

four main races in Singapore. The CDAC is responsible for the low-income Chinese who have low self-esteem and there are other self-help organizations for the Malays and Indians.

The objective of CDAC is to support, foster and promote socio-economic, educational and skills development of the less successful of the Chinese community in Singapore. Its agenda for the year 2008 was to continue to expand its four-plus-three programmes. These are education, skills training and student service centres, volunteers and social services, CDAC workfare and silver talent. It also aims to help students from low-income families to acquire learning tools and attend enrichment programmes through the CDAC opportunity fund.

During the period 1993–2007, CDAC sponsored more than 44,000 workers. CDAC is important in two respects. First, upon receiving relevant training, their incomes will increase. CDAC has found that there is a change in the mindset of some of these recipients in that they will continue to attend training courses for self-improvement. Secondly, CDAC also helps the children of low-income families by providing them with free tuition programmes. These children, who come from a poor learning environment, will get assistance from CDAC, and many of them will then have the opportunity to proceed to ITE for a vocational education.

One of the reasons why CDAC has been able to persuade low-income citizens to enroll and complete their courses is that the monetary incentive is given to them when they complete the course. On the other hand, they are required to pay back the full amount of the subsidy if they cannot complete the course. This CDAC principle is being duplicated in the 2010 Budget which states that low-income Singaporeans will be rewarded up to S$400 a year by the government when they complete their training courses.

The No-One-Is-Left-Behind Strategy is a pillar in Singapore's concerted effort to increase productivity growth nationwide and to promote a harmonious society. Besides, ESS, CDAC and other self-help bodies, the Continuing Education and Training (CET) scheme also runs courses to improve knowledge, raise productivity and instill life-long learning attitudes in adult Singaporeans (Figure 1).

LABOUR MARKET ADJUSTMENT MECHANISMS

No manpower planning, no matter how well-calibrated it is, can ensure that the demand for labour is equal to the supply of labour at both macro and occupational levels. If supply exceeds demand, the wage rate and employment will fall. If there is wage rigidity, the employment level will clear the labour market by falling further. If demand exceeds supply, both the wage rate and employment level will rise. If the employment level is not increased sufficiently, the wage level will increase rapidly, which will trim demand and, in the process, slow down the pace of economic development.

In the case of Singapore, policymakers want to achieve full employment for their citizens and at the same time, have the wage level increase in an orderly manner. In the case of a recession, policy-makers would want to stabilize the employment level, allowing wage costs to fall to clear the labour market. This has been the experience of Singapore because, as Chew and Chew (1992) argue, Singapore has the following built-in adjustment mechanisms which enable labour demand to be bridged by labour supply as part of a self-correcting mechanism.

The Public Sector Mechanism

If labour demand is less than labour supply in the economy, the public sector should employ more. If the private sector is doing very well, the public sector should not compete with the private sector for manpower. Chew and Chew (1992) proposed that the civil service should not be a wage leader for the following reason: when the labour market is tight, few fresh graduates would want to work for the public sector as private sector pay will be higher. During a recession, many fresh graduates would want to work for the public sector as the private sector pay will be lower. But the government was against this idea in the 1990s because, among other reasons, they did not believe in applying Keynesian policy in the labour market.

But the 2008–2009 financial crisis has changed the government's mindset. The 2009 Budget announced that a total of 18,000 public sector jobs would be made available over the following two years. This includes government-supported jobs outside the public sector in areas such as childcare, tertiary education, and restructured hospitals. Under the Ministry of Manpower Professional Skills Programme Traineeship (PSPT) and the Economic Development Board's Preparing for the Upturn (Prep-up) scheme, firms are encouraged to employ fresh graduates by partly or entirely paying their salaries for a period of two years. These two schemes were introduced at the end of 2008. Now in 2010, PSPT is almost redundant.

Strategic Instead of Adversarial Collective Bargaining

In many countries, unions demand higher wage increases without paying much attention to the impact on employment. If management refuses to give in to the wage demand, slow-downs or strikes may be the consequence. This adversarial collective bargaining approach will not benefit the economy and can be a hindrance in Singapore's effort to attract foreign investment (Borgas, 2010). The labour movement in Singapore is represented by the National Trades Union Congress (NTUC). The NTUC takes into account macroeconomic factors in wage negotiations with management. In other words, the NTUC practices strategic collective bargaining under which the unions and the management work together to increase productivity via cooperation and training such that both get higher wages as a result of the higher profits enjoyed by firms (Chew and Chew, 2010a). The union's strategy of facilitating the increase in the size of the profit pie will make the industries more competitive and help to reduce structural unemployment.

The Foreign Labour Mechanism

The foreign labour mechanism should be linked to the needs of the labour market and should promote industrial peace. There are restrictions on employing foreign labour based on a ratio of local workers per foreign worker and the foreign worker levy. Despite high economic growth over successive decades, in the last few years there has been a rise in complaints by locals about the influx of foreign workers and their impact on jobs and wages. Hence, in the 2010 budget, the government wanted to raise productivity mainly because it does not want to rely on foreign workers for future GDP growth.

The Wage Fixing Mechanism

The NWC can influence wage increases in tandem with the direction of the economic restructuring of the economy. The NWC, together with the Industrial Arbitration Court, can influence wage increases at the plant level in the unionized sector. However, NWC's influence on wage increases has been visibly lacking since 1988. Since then, NWC has been more active in non-wage matters such as reform of the wage system and raising of the age of retirement.

The Training Mechanism

SDF is an effective tool in bridging the skill gaps in Singapore because the SDF-sponsored training programmes are chosen by the employers themselves. ITE plays an important role here too. For certain courses, ITE graduates obtain professional certificates apart from ITE certificates. For instance, ITE has signed a Memorandum of Understanding with Adobe, a leading software development agency. For courses in Digital Media Design, Digital Audio and Video Production and Multimedia Technology, Adobe's role is to provide certification for the students and the staff. Hence, ITE graduates in these courses will also get Adobe Certificate Associates ACA certification.

No Free Lunch Mechanism

Everyone in Singapore wants and must work because there is no universal unemployment benefits scheme. There is a well-established literature on the undesirable impact of unemployment benefits schemes on the job search period. With effect from 2013, most employees in Singapore will have a CPF Life account under which a monthly pension payment based on their respective CPF savings will be given at age 65 till death. Apart from CPF there is no pension scheme for the public sector. In Greece and in the Euro zone, civil servants get angry when their governments want to raise the age of retirement but in Singapore employees are usually pleased when the age of retirement is raised. Our non-pension wage system is, therefore, an effective labour market adjustment mechanism.

The Manpower Exchange Mechanism

The Ministry of Manpower keeps a registry of job vacancies and a list of job seekers. This reduces frictional unemployment. Many government agencies such as the five Development Councils also provide the same service and they also prepare applicants for job interviews. Perhaps, the most powerful manpower exchange mechanism is the Employment and Employability Institute (MMI), which is initiated by the NTUC, WDA and Singapore National Employers Federation (SNEF). MMI is a marketplace for employers, jobseekers and training providers as it has a vacancy bank of over 6000 and helps over 14,000 job seekers a year to find new and better jobs. To ensure job seekers meet the hiring requirements of employers, MMI conducts employment coaching and conducts employability and skills training to equip workers with the mindset, skills and job opportunities to stay employable for life. MMI services all segment of workers, from rank and file to professional, managers, executives and technicians.

The Jobs Re-design Mechanism

The Jobs Re-design programme is an effective way to reduce structural unemployment and Singapore's reliance on foreign workers and at the same time provide jobs for local workers. The WDA has various grants to help firms in Singapore to restructure their work processes, etc., with the objective of creating fewer but higher paying jobs.

CHALLENGES AND PROPOSALS

The government in the 2010 Budget stated their intention to set up the National Productivity and Continuing Education Council (NPCEC) to steer the productivity drive. The fact that the NPCEC is chaired by the Deputy Prime Minister of Singapore shows that the Singapore government is fully determined and committed to increase national productivity growth.

While the operating principles of the NPCEC are yet to be ironed out, it is proposed that the NPCEC work closely with the NWC because the productivity campaign can only be sustained if it is explicitly linked to wage increases since wage growth is directly linked to productivity growth.

Singaporeans will support the principle of wage growth on two conditions: there must be productivity growth every year and the inflation rate must be low. The role of all citizens, workers, labour unions, firms, public institutions and government ministries is to raise productivity. The role of the government is twofold: to facilitate the national productivity drive and to keep the inflation rate low. If there is high inflation due to external forces, the government will help the poor by implementing fiscal policies and firms will give one-time lump sum payments to low-income workers, all of which have been done before. This new social contract will generate an increase in real income and the standard of living for all citizens for many years to come on a sustainable basis.

It can be expected that the Singapore economy will face shorter business cycles in an increasingly competitive global market for exports and foreign investment. Management of the labour market for competitiveness is even more important for a small open economy such as Singapore. The current painful experience of Greece shows that there is no free lunch. If an economic policy is not sustainable but is nevertheless implemented, every citizen will suffer ultimately. On the other hand, due to shorter and more volatile business cycles, the poor will feel more pain during a downturn. Fiscal measures have to support the poor during a downtown when government revenue falls. This means that over the cycle, the government must operate a budget surplus. As the experience of the Euro-zone shows, bad labour market policies are the main cause of persistent budget deficits (James, 2010). The Singapore government can enjoy annual budget surplus because of Singapore's healthy labour market practices.

END NOTES

Borgas, G (2010). *Labour Economics* (Fifth Edition). New York: McGraw-Hill.

Chew, R and S B Chew (2005). Wage issues and human resources in Singapore. *Journal of Comparative Asian Development*, 4(1), 77–103.

Chew, R and S B Chew (2010a). From Adversarial Collective Bargaining to Strategic Collective Bargaining, mimeo.

Chew, S B and R Chew (1992). *The Singapore Worker: A Profile*. Singapore: Oxford University Press.

Chew, S B and R Chew (2008). Macro objectives of the central provident fund: A review. In Chia Wai Mun and Sng Hui Ying (eds.), *Singapore and Asia in a Globalised World*, Singapore: World Scientific, pp. 35–62.

Chew, S B and R Chew (2010b). Youth employment and training in Singapore. *Bulletin of Comparative Labour Relations*, 73, 119–134.

James, H (2010). Euro's woes: Don't just blame Greece. *Straits Times*, 6 March.

Lim, C Y and Associates (1988). *The Singapore Economy: Policy Options*. Singapore: McGraw-Hill.

Lim, C Y and R Chew (1998). *Wages and Wages Policies Tripartism in Singapore*. Singapore: World Scientific.

Ministry of Finance (2009). *Keep Jobs, Building for the Future*. Singapore, Ministry of Finance, Budget Speech, 2009.

Ministry of Finance (2010). *Towards An Advanced Economy: Superior Skills, Quality Jobs, Higher Incomes*. Singapore, Ministry of Finance, Budget Speech 2010.

Sheng, A (2009). *From Asian to Global Financial Crisis*. Singapore: Cambridge University Press.

Chapter 6

CHINA AS AN EMERGING MARKET FOR SINGAPORE: CHALLENGES AND OPPORTUNITIES

Yunhua Liu

INTRODUCTION

The outstanding post-crisis performance of the Chinese economy has not only surprised the world but has persuaded many countries to readjust their expectations and orient their economic policies towards China. With a steady expansion of trade and investment activities with China over the past decade, Singapore has successfully integrated with the newly merged huge market. How far will Singapore benefit from further trade and investment with China? What are the challenges which the Chinese market will pose for Singapore policymakers? These are some of the questions which will be the focus of this chapter.

In the early 1990s and into the present century, China competed with Singapore in both manufactured exports and for foreign direct investment (FDI) but this has now changed as Singapore successfully moved up the value-added chain and matured into a more developed economy. The relationship is now more complementary than competitive but China still offers opportunities which Singapore can take advantage of as it strives to maintain the momentum of economic growth.

CHALLENGES TO SINGAPORE FROM THE RISE OF CHINA

The challenges facing Singapore from the rise of China in the 1990s and 2000s were relatively clear in terms of competition in third country markets for exports of manufactured goods and as rival destinations for foreign direct investment. However, since Singapore has successfully moved up the value chain this rivalry has become less prominent. The challenge for Singapore now is to integrate more closely with the Chinese economy.

Competition in World Export Markets

Given the growth of world demand for labor intensive goods in the past ten years, fast expansion of China's exports has inevitably taken market share away from traditional labor intensive exporting countries. As China began to source a large proportion of its imports from Hong Kong and Taiwan, two traditional competitors of Singapore, other Newly-Industrialized Countries (NIEs) were the most affected. Table 1 shows Singapore maintained a steady market share in the US of around 2.5% in the early 1990s, but this share fell steadily after 1997 to reach 1.92% in 2000, while China's share of the US market has increased continuously. From 2004 onwards, US imports from Singapore remained fairly constant but there was a sharp rise in imports from China, reaching US$273 billion by 2008 with a market share 13%.

Table 1: US imports from Singapore, China and the World 1987–2008

	World US$ billion	Singapore	Share %	China US$ billion	Share %
1987	409.7	7.30	1.78	3.10	0.76
1988	447.1	9.50	2.12	3.50	0.78
1989	477.6	10.7	2.24	4.70	0.98
1990	498.4	11.7	2.35	5.80	1.16
1991	491.0	11.9	2.42	6.80	1.38
1992	536.5	13.6	2.53	9.60	1.79
1993	589.4	15.1	2.56	18.4	3.12
1994	668.7	17.6	2.63	22.5	3.36
1995	749.3	21.2	2.83	26.0	3.47
1996	803.1	23.2	2.89	28.9	3.60
1997	876.8	23.1	2.63	35.4	4.04
1998	918.6	22.0	2.39	41.2	4.49
1999	1034.3	22.6	2.19	47.4	4.58
2000	1230.4	23.6	1.92	62.3	5.06
2004	1485.5	23.3	1.57	125.1	8.42
2005	1692.8	23.9	1.41	163.3	9.65
2006	1875.3	27.6	1.47	203.9	10.87
2007	1983.5	26.6	1.34	233.2	11.76
2008	2139.5	22.9	1.07	273.1	12.76

Sources: U.S. Census Bureau, Foreign Trade Division for U.S. Data. Asian Development Bank, for Singapore and China Data.

Competition for Inward FDI

Singapore has always been an attractive destination for foreign direct investment but has been eclipsed by China in recent years. In 1997 the Republic attracted US$13.5 billion of FDI while China received US$44.2 billion in absolute terms. However, by 2002 these amounts were US$7.7 billion and US$52.7, respectively. By 2006 the amount for Singapore was US$29 billion while that for China had risen rapidly to around US$70 billion (Table 2).

There is no doubt that there has been a substantial diversion of FDI from Southeast Asia to China. Table 2 shows the amount of FDI going to Singapore and China over the past three decades.

Table 2:   Foreign direct investment inflows into China and Singapore 1980–2006.

US$ million	China	Singapore	Year	China	Singapore
1980	57	1,236	1995	35,849	11,503
1981	265	1,660	1996	40,180	9,303
1982	430	1,602	1997	44,237	13,533
1983	636	1,134	1998	43,751	7,594
1984	1,258	1,302	1999	40,319	13,245
1985	1,659	1,047	2000	40,772	12,464
1986	1,875	1,710	2001	46,846	10,949
1987	2,314	2,836	2002	52,700	7,655
1988	3,194	3,655	2003	53,500	10,376
1989	3,393	2,887	2004	60,600	14,819
1990	3,487	5,575	2005	60,300	20,081
1991	4,366	4,887	2006	69,500	29,000
1992	11,156	2,204			
1993	27,515	4,686			
1994	33,787	8,550			

Sources: World Trade Analyzer CDROM, 2001, International Monetary Fund, *International Financial Statistics*, 2001 and http://www.uschina.org/statistics/fdi_cumulative.html.

Historically, Singapore has relied on FDI heavily for its economic growth and industrialization and in absolute terms the inflow to Singapore only fell behind China significantly after 1991. Since 2003, however, FDI inflows into Singapore have increased again due to improvements in the investment environment in Singapore, such as the reduction in the corporate tax rate, a fall in labor costs and better infrastructure. So Singapore is no longer dwarfed by China.

THE INCREASING IMPORTANCE OF THE CHINA MARKET TO SINGAPORE

Table 3 shows the change in the destination of Singapore's exports over the last nineteen years. China is now the fastest growing market for Singapore's exports. Between 1990 and 2008, the annual average

Table 3: Direction of Singapore's exports and imports 1990–2008

US$ billion	1990	1995	2000	2004	2005	2006	2007	2008	Annual average growth rate %
Total exports	52.8	118.2	138.1	198.9	229.7	272.5	299.8	347.5	11.0
Malaysia	6.8	22.6	25.0	27.2	30.4	35.5	38.6	43.8	10.9
Hong Kong	3.4	10.1	10.8	17.6	21.5	27.5	31.3	37.0	14.2
Indonesia	—	—	—	19.0	22.1	24.9	29.4	38.4	—
USA	11.2	21.5	23.8	23.2	23.8	27.6	26.6	22.8	4.0
China, P.R.	0.7	2.7	5.3	15.3	19.7	26.5	28.9	32.9	23.8
Japan	4.6	9.2	10.4	11.5	12.5	14.8	14.3	15.5	7.0
Thailand	3.4	6.8	5.8	7.7	9.4	11.3	12.3	12.3	7.4
Australia	1.3	2.5	3.2	6.6	8.4	10.1	11.1	14.3	14.2
Korea	1.1	3.2	4.9	7.3	8.0	8.7	10.6	13.1	14.7
India	1.1	1.8	2.8	4.1	5.8	7.6	10.0	12.3	14.4
Total imports	60.9	124.4	134.6	172.6	200.1	238.7	263.3	330.9	9.9
Malaysia	8.2	19.2	22.8	24.9	27.3	31.1	34.4	40.5	9.3
USA	9.8	18.7	20.2	20.7	23.4	30.3	32.8	36.6	7.6
China, P.R.	2.0	4.0	7.1	16.2	20.5	27.2	31.8	35.9	17.4
Japan	12.2	26.3	23.1	19.0	19.2	19.9	21.5	26.6	4.4
Indonesia	—	—	—	9.7	10.4	14.7	14.6	18.3	—
Korea	1.7	5.3	4.8	6.9	8.5	10.4	12.8	19.1	14.4
Saudi Arabia	3.2	3.7	4.3	5.0	8.9	9.2	8.8	15.5	9.2
Thailand	1.6	6.4	5.8	6.7	7.5	8.7	8.4	10.9	11.2
Germany	2.1	4.3	4.2	5.6	5.9	6.8	8.1	9.0	8.4
France	1.4	2.7	2.1	4.1	3.8	5.3	6.1	7.9	11.1

Source: Asian Development Bank, *Key Indicators, 2009*.

growth rate of Singapore's exports to China was 23.8%. Indeed, taken together, Hong Kong and Mainland China now account for more than 20% of Singapore's total exports, which far overweighs Singapore's exports to the USA. Together with Hong Kong, the other fast-growing markets include Korea, India and Australia. On the other hand exports to the US and Japanese markets grew by only 4% and 7%, respectively.

A second feature of Singapore's trade with China is its increased complementarity. More often than not, Singapore has recorded a trade deficit with China in the past ten years. This is a reflection of China's diversified resources, products and technology, which supply Singapore with consumption goods and production parts.

The change in the composition of Singapore's major merchandise exports to China between 1990 and 2000 indicates that machinery and transport equipment have taken over from minerals fuels, lubricants and related materials (largely petroleum and petroleum products) as the top export category (Table 4). As can be seen in the table, electrical machinery, apparatus and appliances accounted for about a quarter of Singapore's exports to China in 2000, a tremendous increase compared to 1990. This reflects the growing connections between Singapore and China as Singaporean firms invest in China and China becomes a more attractive production base for electronics products.

However, China is also demanding electronics components from Singapore. According to the Singapore Ministry of Trade and Industry (Chua, 2001), China imports a large part of the electronics components that it uses, thus Singapore's exporters can benefit from the growth of electronic components industries in China. China imported a total of US$14 billion worth of semiconductors in 2000 and only exported US$3 billion worth. Even though Singapore's exports of end products are dwindling, Singapore can play the role of a supplier of sophisticated, highly specialized electronic components to firms involved in other electronics production in the region, especially in China. The rise of the electronics industry in the region can also benefit Singapore's domestic exports of chemical products used in the manufacture of electronics goods.

Table 4: Singapore's major merchandise exports to China, 1990 and 2000

SITC category	Export share (% of total exports to China)	
	1990	2000
7-Machinery and transport equipment	16.0	57.8
77-Electrical machinery, apparatus & appliances	1.8	25.6
75-Office machines & automatic data processing	1.3	19.5
3-Mineral fuels, lubricants and related materials	39.4	14.0
33-Petroleum, petroleum products and related materials	39.0	13.2
5-Chemicals and related products, n.e.s	15.0	14.5
58-Artif. Resins, plastic materials, cellulose esters	9.5	7.7
8-Miscellaneous manufactured articles	3.3	6.1
6-Manufactured goods classified chiefly by material	4.9	4.5

Source: World Trade Analyzer CD-ROM and Author's computations.

Initially when China began to open up its trade and investment to the world there was some concern in the Asian region that China could become a threat to other countries, both politically and economically. However the reality has been very different. The strong demand for investment and consumption in the fast growing Chinese economy has been a powerful stimulus to regional exports from countries as diverse as Malaysia, Japan and Singapore and an important countercyclical stabilizer during the present global financial crisis. Indeed the support provided by Chinese growth and import demand from the region has continued after the crisis.

Going forward, China's participation in the World Trade Organization and in free trade agreements with other Asian countries should lead to further tariff and non-tariff barriers coming down in the region to the benefit of intra-Asian trade and investment flows. For Singapore, a model estimated by Liu (2007) shows a clear inverse relationship between the reduction of the average tariff rate in a specific industry (TR) and Singapore's exports to China measured in thousands of US dollars (EX). The model also includes the Yuan/S$ exchange rate (ER). The equation was estimated between 1987 and

Table 5: Tariff effects for different products in Singapore's exports to China, 1987–2000

Products	N^*	a_2
Primary goods (sitc 0,1,2,3,4)	168	−732.63 (−1.88)
Food & beverages (sitc 00–12)	72	392.32 (2.26)
Crude materials (sitc 21–43)	96	−2537.54 (−2.49)
Manufactures (sitc 5,6,7,8,9)	210	−602.82 (−1.56)
Chemical & related (sitc 51–59)	54	60.31 (0.15)
Basic manufactures (sitc 61–69)	54	−153.08 (−2.30)
Machines, transport (sitc 71–79)	54	−636.27 (−2.33)
Miscellaneous manufactured (sitc 81–89)	48	−168.58 (−2.54)

Note: N^* is the number of observations and the numbers in parentheses are *t*-values.

2000 using data from the United Nations Standard International Trade Classification (SITC).

$$EX = a_0 + a_1 ER + a_2 TR + a_3 YEAR + u$$

The results are presented in Table 5. Clearly Singapore has benefited substantially across a range of manufacturing categories from a one per cent tariff reduction in China as the average tariff rate fell from 11.3% in 2000 to 9% by the end of the 5th year of China's WTO entry. After the China-ASEAN free trade agreement was established in 2010, tariffs should be removed completely. The largest benefit, however, is for crude materials, which is Singapore's refined oil exports. If tariffs are eventually removed entirely the total stimulus to Singapore's exports should be substantial. Note that the exchange rate effect is ambiguous due to the pegged exchange rate policy of China in the earlier years but the adoption of a managed floating regime in 2005 and gradual appreciation of the yuan may have had a positive effect on Singapore's exports to China.

SINGAPORE'S INVESTMENT IN CHINA

Following the 1985–1986 recession in Singapore policies were enacted to encourage firms located in Singapore to venture abroad and 'sprout a second wing' in order to diversify the sources of Singapore's incomes from international trade and investment. As a result China became one of the main destinations for Singapore's investment due to its abundant labor and land and huge market potential. One early initiative was the development of a 'model' industrial park in Suzhou and this has been followed by a biotech City in Tianjin and 'Knowledge Cities' in Nanjing and Guangzhou.

As at end 2006, China, Malaysia and Indonesia were Singapore's top Asian investment destinations. China is still Singapore's top invest-ment destination, with total direct investment reaching US$30.7 billion (Table 6). Singapore is now the largest investor in China after Hong Kong, Taiwan, the USA and Japan. Singapore's investment in China mostly goes into manufacturing (64.1%) and real estate, rental and leasing services (13%) and according to the China Development Gateway on December 28th 2008,[61] major recipients of Singapore's investment include machinery, industrial and agricultural production and food processing, rubber, textiles, electronics, steel and real estate.

For Singapore investing in China has been a learning process. Early investment in the Suzhou Industrial Park, which was heavily funded by the Singapore government, was costly and the results were somewhat disappointing, partly because of communications problems

Table 6: Singapore's total direct investment in China 1997, 1998 and 2006

Year	Total S$ (million)	% Distribution by activity within China				
		Manufacturing (%)	Commerce (%)	Financial (%)	Real estate (%)	Business services (%)
1997	10,477	60	5.5	3	21	1
1998	11,593	61	7	3	20	1
2006	30,698	64	—	—	13	—

Source: Singapore: *Department of Statistics.*

---

[61] Economic and Trade Relations between China and Singapore, retrieved from http://www.chinagate.com.cn/english/366.htm.

between Singapore and the local and central government authorities and a general lack of understanding about how to deal with Chinese officials. Since then, however, substantial progress has been made, helped by the decision to send young Singaporean officials to China rather than just investors.

CONCLUSION

The emergence of China has provided Singapore with a broad and dynamic market in trade and investment activity. The challenge for Singapore is to manage the integration of the Singapore economy with Chinese economy smoothly.

END NOTES

Chew, S B and Y Liu (1998). Competition in trade between China and ASEAN. *Advances in Pacific Basin Business, Economics and Finance*, 3, 141–159.

Chua, B L (2001). *Declining Global Market Shares of Singapore's Electronics Exports: Is It a Concern?* Singapore: Ministry of Trade and Industry.

Liu, Y (2007). Facing the challenge of rising China: Singapore's responses. *Journal of Policy Modeling*, 29, 505–522.

Chapter

7

EQUITY IN SINGAPORE'S HEALTHCARE FINANCING[62]

Tilak Abeysinghe, Himani, and Jeremy Lim

INTRODUCTION

Within a short span of time since independence in 1965, Singapore has not only produced high GDP growth rates, but has also succeeded in translating high growth into remarkable health achievements. Singapore's healthcare indicators are among the best in the world today. The infant mortality rate, which stood above 35 per 1000 live births in 1960, had fallen to 2.1 by 2007. Such very low rates (below 3) were recorded only for Luxembourg (1.8), Iceland (2.0), Sweden (2.5), Japan (2.6) and Finland (2.6).[63]

---

[62] An earlier version of this chapter was presented at the Singapore Economic Policy Conference held on October 27, 2009 at the Hyatt Hotel, Singapore and the authors would like to thank the conference participants for their comments.

[63] OECD Health Data, 2009, available online at www.ecosante.org.

What is even more remarkable is that Singapore achieved this by spending relatively less on healthcare compared to almost every other developed country. Singapore has consistently spent less than 4% of its GDP on healthcare while in 2007 Luxembourg spent 7.3%, Iceland 9.3%, Sweden 9.1%, Japan 8.1% and Finland 8.2%. Channeling high growth into better housing, clean water, improved sanitation and good education when combined with better nutrition and preventive healthcare has made it possible for Singapore to improve the health status of its population while spending a small portion of GDP on direct healthcare.

In 2000, the World Health Organization (2000) ranked Singapore sixth out of 191 countries in terms of overall performance in healthcare based on the criteria of health status (both level and distribution), responsiveness (both level and distribution), equity, and efficiency (achievement per dollar spent). We gain more insight into the performance of a country by paying attention to these components. Some data extracted from the WHO report are reproduced in Table 1, which shows the top 10 countries based on their overall ranking, plus the UK, Australia, and the USA for comparison. Note the ranking for Oman, which is 8th in terms of overall performance, but it is lowest in the table in terms of health status, responsiveness and per capita health expenditure, and second lowest in terms of equity (fairness in financial contribution). Therefore, the overall ranking which measures the overall attainment relative to per dollar spent (efficiency) is quite misleading in this case.

As for Singapore, what is immediately noticeable in the table is that in terms of equity Singapore gets a very distant rank of 101–102, despite its overall ranking of sixth. Again caution has to be exercised in interpreting this ranking. The lower equity ranking is a result of Singapore's larger out-of-pocket expenditure share in healthcare financing (see footnote 67). However, the actual dollar amount for the same treatment in Singapore could be much lower than, for example, in the US. Nevertheless, these results suggest that Singapore in general scores very highly in terms of efficiency but not so well as far as the equity of financing health expenditures is concerned.

Table 1: World Health Organization 2000 rankings

Member state	ATTAINMENT OF GOALS						PERFORMANCE		
	Health status		Responsiveness		Fairness in financial contribution	Overall	Health spending per capita	Level of health	Overall
	Level	Dist.	Level	Dist.					
France	3	12	16–17	3–38	26–29	6	4	4	1
Italy	6	14	22–23	3–38	45–47	11	11	3	2
San Marino	11	9	32	3–38	30–32	21	21	5	3
Andorra	10	25	28	39–42	33–34	17	23	7	4
Malta	21	38	43–44	3–38	42–44	31	37	2	5
Singapore	**30**	**29**	**20–21**	**3–38**	**101–102**	**27**	**38**	**14**	**6**
Spain	5	11	34	3–38	26–29	19	24	6	7
Oman	72	59	83	49	56–57	59	62	1	8
Austria	17	8	12–13	3–38	12–15	10	6	15	9
Japan	1	3	6	3–38	8–11	1	13	9	10
UK	14	2	26–27	3–38	8–11	9	26	24	18
Australia	2	17	12–13	3–38	26–29	12	17	39	32
USA	24	32	1	3–38	54–55	15	1	72	37

Note: Dist = distribution. Ranking is based on 191 countries.
Source: World Health Organization (2000).

As Table 1 highlights, two extreme healthcare financing systems are the UK and the USA. The tax-based single payer universal healthcare system in the UK scores highly on equity grounds but the problems of long waiting lists, rationing and the intergenerational transfer of tax burden have made the UK system less attractive. The problems of the insurance-based less equitable US system are well known and took the center stage in President Obama's policy reform agenda. In the midst of these discussions Singapore's well-functioning healthcare system has attracted a lot of attention worldwide.[64]

Given this background, the key question is whether Singapore should be concerned about the equity issue at all? The objective of this chapter is to address this question. After a brief review of Singapore's healthcare financing system, including a review of the literature that tries to critically evaluate Singapore's medical savings accounts system, we present a summary of the results from a data analysis based on hospital expenditure of a large pool of elderly Singaporeans. Finally, we highlight the general observations that emerge from this analysis with regard to equity and adequacy. As Singaporeans become more vocal the equity issue in healthcare financing will become more important and in the last Section we make some suggestions with the objective of achieving more equitable results under a more comprehensive insurance cover without unduly burdening the tax base.

SINGAPORE'S HEALTHCARE FINANCING SYSTEM

Singapore's healthcare is provided by both the public and the private sector.[65] The National Health Plan (NHP) of 1983 and the White Paper on affordable healthcare of 1993 are the two key health policy documents in Singapore (Phua, 1991; Reisman, 2006; Asher and

---

[64] For a long list of the accolades that the Singapore health system has received, See the Singapore Ministry of Health website (www.moh.gov.sg). The problem of looking after the poor and elderly poor in Singapore's 'individual responsibility system' is also addressed in Chapter 11.

[65] For a more detailed account of the healthcare system in Singapore, readers are referred to www.moh.gov.sg.

Nandy, 2006). Both these documents emphasize individual responsibility as the cornerstone of the country's healthcare financing philosophy. Besides the individual, the family is adjudged to have a "primary" responsibility in caring for the aged. While promoting individual responsibility through a co-payment system, providing affordable healthcare to all Singaporeans is an essential ingredient of the public healthcare financing scheme.

To help Singaporeans pay their medical expenses, the government introduced compulsory medical savings, known as Medisave, in 1984. The rationale behind the savings approach adopted by the government is that the current generation of wage-earners should save for their healthcare needs in old age instead of relying on uncertain tax revenues from future generations. Thus, the system should not place an unduly heavy burden on the declining number of the young and productive. Moreover, it was believed that this system would generate efficiency gains by restraining the overconsumption of health services which is a common feature of third-party financing schemes (Lim, 2004).

Two complementary schemes, Medishield and Medifund, were implemented at a later date. Medishield is a low cost, relatively high deductible, catastrophic health insurance scheme introduced in 1990 to help patients cope with unusually high hospitals bills. The premiums can be paid using Medisave balances. The government has continuously reformed Medishield by expanding both its coverage and benefits. Medisave and Medishield operate within a broader government-regulated compulsory savings scheme called the Central Provident Fund (CPF).

Medifund was established in 1993 to ensure that essential medical treatment is not denied to Singaporeans who face financial hardship as judged by means testing. Thus, it acts as a safety net for citizens who are unable to pay their hospital expenses despite Medisave, Medishield and government subsidies. In addition to the "3M" system (Medisave, Medishield, Medifund), a special insurance scheme for the elderly, Eldershield, was launched in September 2002. It covers long-term care associated with severe disabilities in old age. As with Medishield, it is an opt-out scheme and premiums can be deducted from Medisave.

As well as these schemes, government subsidies, financed through general taxation, play a crucial role in financing hospital costs. The government's policy of price discrimination, based on different ward classes in public hospitals, ranges in ascending order of comfort from class C through to B2, B1 and A. This allows subsidies to be targeted at poorer users based on individual choice of amenities. In January 2009, the government introduced a means testing scheme for class C and B2 ward admissions to ensure that the public subsidies go to the most financially deserving. A summary of the healthcare financing system is presented in Figure 1 and the government subsidy scheme through the ward-class system is detailed in Table 2. Further details can be obtained from the Ministry of Health website cited above.

The medical savings accounts (MSA) scheme of Singapore has attracted both praise and concern on the grounds of cost containment, equity and adequacy. Proponents of the MSA argue that it checks overutilization of health services by creating cost-conscious consumers. Thus, it eliminates efficiency losses arising from moral hazard associated with third-party pre-paid systems and contains rising health costs, which has become a major problem in the developed world (Massaro and Wong, 1995; Pauly, 2001; Eiff *et al.*, 2002). Others have argued

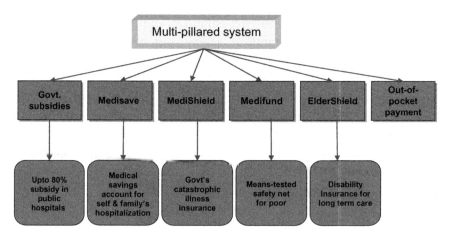

Figure 1:   The structure of Singapore's healthcare financing system.

Table 2: Singapore Government subsidies and the ward-class system

Ward type	Subsidy	Beds per room	Attached toilet & shower	Air-con	T.V. & phone
A	0	1	Yes	Yes	Yes
B1	20%	4	Yes	Yes	Yes
B2+	50%	5	Yes	Yes	No
B2	50–65%	6	No	No	No
C	65–80%	>6 (open ward)	No	No	No

that the main policy objective of the MSA scheme is not cost-containment but to mobilize non-budgetary resources to help pay for the increasing medical expenditure expected from a rapidly aging population. This resolves the problem of intergenerational transfers that a rapidly ageing society poses in a tax-financed system. With this shift in public cost-sharing, government tax revenue can be freed to address other concerns (Prescott and Nichols, 1997; Phua and Yap, 1998).

There are others who doubt the scheme's ability to curtail costs. Hsiao (1995) argues that the MSA scheme cannot contain healthcare costs in Singapore and this realization has led the government to consider supply side measures, such as, regulating the supply of hospital beds and physicians, to reduce provider-induced demand. Barr (2001) attributes Singapore's low healthcare spending to strict government control of inputs and outputs, rationing based on wealth and to social and demographic features peculiar to the Republic. He asserts that the MSA plays a minor role in the Singapore healthcare system. Shortt (2002) argues that the demand-side approach contained in MSA is not effective in controlling healthcare costs without the supply side regulations.

These writers have also criticized the MSA system for promoting inequities in society. Barr (2001) claims that: "For most of the population, the cost of moving outside the parameters set by the 3Ms in Singapore is prohibitive. Chronically sick, the working poor and the elderly, particularly old women, are seriously disadvantaged". Shortt (2002) notes that Medisave, especially when coupled with tax advantages, benefits the healthy and wealthy while leaving the sick either to seek higher cost comprehensive insurance or to bear increased out-of-pocket expenses. Shortt also claims that "health care costs in Singapore often cannot be met by elderly people, especially elderly widows who were never employed outside the home, and poor people". In the same vein, Asher and Nandy (2006) have argued that the tax treatment of Medisave exacerbates the regressive nature of the health financing system. The exemption of contributions from income tax, interest income and withdrawals from Medisave, does not benefit two-thirds of the labor force that does not pay income tax.

The claims by Barr (2001) and Shortt (2002) are, however, made in the absence of any real data. Chia and Tsui (2005), by contrast, use survey data of a longitudinal study of transition in health and wealth of elderly Singaporeans to assess the adequacy of their medical savings to finance their medical expenses over the post retirement period. They estimate the present value of lifetime healthcare expenses of Singaporeans upon retirement. Their results show that the minimum Medisave sum would be adequate for both the less well off male and female elderly at 4% increase in medical costs and at a discount rate of 4% or higher. It is also adequate for better-off male elderly but not for female elderly. The shortfall is in the range of 34–75% of the minimum sum and becomes more severe when medical expenses grow at higher rates. Note that the findings of the Chia-Tsui study are based on the respondents' account of their health expenses in the previous year. In the next section we present some results based on *actual* hospital bills of a large pool of elderly Singaporeans to address some issues pertaining to equity and adequacy.

HEALTHCARE EXPENDITURE OF ELDERLY SINGAPOREANS[66]

The data for the analysis were extracted from hospital bills of the elderly (64 years and above) admitted to a tertiary public hospital

---

[66] The data analysis was carried out by the second author as part of her PhD thesis.

throughout 2007. The information gathered include itemized inpatient expenses and modes of financing, inpatient's characteristics such as age, gender, length of stay, diagnoses (primary and secondary) and outcome of hospitalization. The sample size used for the analysis consists of 30,192 hospitalization episodes of 18,935 elderly patients.

There is a huge variation in expenditure across ward classes due to government subsidies. Table 3 shows the distribution of bill size by ward class. The expenditure distribution is highly skewed with a long right tail. The data show that the patients in different wards received an average government subsidy amounting to 72.4% in C ward, 64.3% in B2 ward, 53.6% in B2+ ward, 13.6% in B1 ward and 0.3% in A ward. The large jump in the bill size for wards A and B over C is immediately noticeable. These two wards were 5.5 and 4.5 times more expensive than ward C. Ward B2+ was 1.6 times more expensive and B2 was only 1.2 times more expensive than C. This explains the popularity of the B2 ward as reflected by the largest sample size for B2 in the table. Just as with the expenditure distribution, the distribution of the length of stay in hospital is skewed to the right (Table 4).

The table also shows that the length of stay in C ward is systematically longer than in other wards across the entire distribution. This is due to a combination of factors: greater subsidies incentivize longer stay; the general health of this low-income stratum of the society is poor; more retired elderly patients choose C ward while the economically active young choose other wards; long-staying patients with

Table 3: Distribution of bill size in Singapore dollars by ward class

Ward class	Sample size	Mean	Median	90th percentile	95th percentile	99th percentile
A	1,395	8,108	4,180	18,326	23,266	48,793
B1	2,324	6,560	3,574	14,819	18,404	33,646
B2+	822	2,305	1,804	4,074	5,681	10,851
B2	15,260	1,727	986	3,989	5,257	10,083
C	10,391	1,466	842	3,257	4,431	9,004
Total	30,192	2,320	1,087	4,778	8,133	19,126

Table 4:   Distribution of length of stay (days) by ward class

Ward class	Mean	Median	90th percentile	95th percentile	99th percentile
A	6.9	4	15	25	53
B1	6.4	4	13	20	39
B2+	5.4	3	11	18	36
B2	6.7	4	15	22	44
C	8.6	5	19	28	57
Total	7.3	4	16	24	49

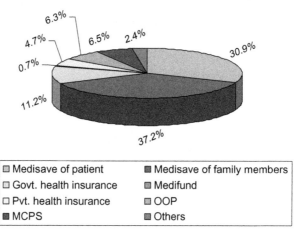

Figure 2:   Payment shares by mode of financing.

Notes: MCPS = Medical Claims Pro-ration & Processing System, OOP = out-of-pocket.

large bills opt to downgrade to C ward; short-staying elective surgical patients choose B2 and higher wards. Maternity wards are also factored into B2 and higher wards, hence shorter stays.

With this background information on the distribution of inpatient expenditure and length of stay, we now move on to examine how inpatient expenditure is financed. The pie chart in Figure 2 shows the shares of different modes of financing hospitalization episodes. Medisave of the patient and family members and out-of-pocket expenditure account for about 75% of hospital bills.[67] This means a B2 ward patient with the average bill of S$1,727 (Table 3) paid S$1,295 from personal and family savings. The contribution of insurance, both government and private, is fairly small, covering only 15% of the bill.

Medisave

In our sample, 55% of the elderly used Medisave to pay for hospitalization. In general, the role of Medisave in financing inpatient expenses of the elderly has been rather modest. This stems partially from the fact that the present cohort of the elderly did not have enough working years left to build up sufficient Medisave balances after the scheme was launched in 1984. As a result, Medisave balances of a large majority of the elderly fall short of the minimum sum stipulated by the government. For example, in 2005 the average Medisave balance of 65 years and older was S$5,300 while the minimum sum required was S$27,500.

Furthermore, due to higher medical needs of the elderly, there has been greater draw-down of their Medisave balances but without matching replenishment. Those who used Medisave paid 71% of C ward costs, 73% of B2 costs, 76% of B2+ costs, 37% of B1 costs and 22% of A ward expenses out of Medisave. More males than females (66% versus 46%) used Medisave to offset their medical bills. The gender difference in Medisave utilization can be explained by the fact that women, due to low paying jobs in the informal sector or unpaid labor such as caregiving and domestic work during their productive years, could accumulate less Medisave balances compared to their male counterparts.

Government Health Insurance (Medishield) and Catastrophic Expenditure

Only 22% of the elderly were covered by Medishield. Older elderly (≥80 years) have very poor insurance coverage (4.4%) while

---

[67] In WHO studies out-of-pocket expenditure refers to what is directly paid out of personal income to settle a hospital bill. By this definition the entire 75% should be counted as out-of-pocket expenditure.

130 T. Abeysinghe et al.

younger elderly (64–74) fare a bit better (28.9%). The negligible coverage of the older elderly could be due to the following reasons. First, the last entry age for Medishield is 75 years though the coverage is up to 85. Second, relatively high premiums and deductibles for older elderly (≥80 years) compared to younger elderly (<80 years) may work as a disincentive to stay in Medishield. The premium jumps from S$524 for 76–78 years and S$615 for 79–80 years to S$1,087 for 81–83 years and S$1,123 for 84–85 years. The deductible is higher for older elderly. For class C ward, the deductible is S$1,000 for 80 years and below while it is S$2,000 for 81–85 years. For the insured elderly, Medishield covered 52% of the bill of a hospitalization episode with vast differences across wards (C 59%, B2 55%, B2+ 33%, B1 15%, and A 11%).

It should be noted that the motivation behind the introduction of Medishield is to protect individuals against catastrophic health expenses. The question remains, nevertheless, how well these insurance alternatives protect the elderly against high (and perhaps catastrophic) expenses, which is a story about the tail of the expenditure distribution. Figure 3 presents the inpatient expenditure distribution cut off at S$5,000. The actual tail extends much longer with a few episodes running beyond $100,000 and a maximum running above $200,000. For the most expensive 10% of episodes, Medishield covered 40% of expenses for the insured elderly with sharp variations across wards. Nearly 68% of the bill was covered in class C ward as against 11% in class A ward. Worth noting is that private health insurance offsets a higher fraction (61%) of hospitalization costs in the top decile than Medishield. Moreover, for private insurance the variation across wards is not as marked as for Medishield where 78% of the bill was covered in class C ward and 53% in class A. We further examined the tail probabilities of predicting catastrophic expenditures by fitting conditional log-normal and Pareto distributions. The objective is, given a diagnosis and other relevant information of a patient, to predict the probability of expenditure exceeding an affordable cut off level. Some findings will be discussed below.

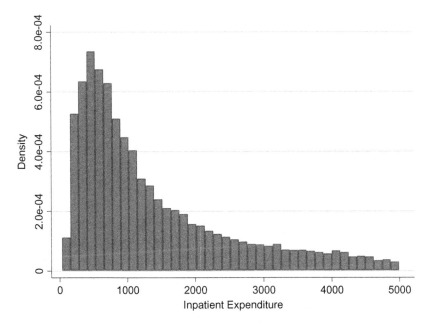

Figure 3: Histogram plot of elderly inpatient expenditure 2007.

Private Health Insurance

Private health insurance is even less popular among the elderly as just 8% of them are covered and older elderly have almost no private insurance. Possible reasons behind the poor take-up of private insurance include a last entry age between 65 and 75 years, high premiums, high deductibles and pre-existing conditions. For the insured elderly private insurance finances about 62% of the expenses of a hospitalization episode.

Medifund

Medifund assistance is only for admissions into ward classes B2 and C. A very small percentage of episodes receive Medifund assistance- only 0.19% in B2 ward and 2.5% in C ward. In fact, less than 1% of the elderly in our sample were helped by Medifund. This low proportion is a consequence of the government's policy to restrict Medifund's role as the last-resort safety net. For those who obtained aid, about three-quarters of expenses of a hospitalization episode were paid from the fund with 51% for B2 ward and 78% for C.

Medisave of Family Members

Despite relatively small contributions by Medisave and insurance in financing hospitalization expenses, average out-of-pocket payments for the elderly was quite small at about 6%, 4.5% for C, B2 and B2+ wards, 18% for B1 and 20% for A wards. The answer to this puzzle lies in a unique feature of Singapore's healthcare financing system wherein Medisave can be used to pay for hospitalization of immediate family members. This is in accordance with the government's initiative to promote the primacy of family in care giving for the elderly. In fact, medical savings of children have become an important source of financing for their elderly parents' healthcare. In terms of our data, 51% of the elderly have their hospital bills paid from their family members' Medisave. More females (64%) than males (38%) tap on family members' medical savings as they have lower Medisave balances and lower insurance coverage than males. For the same reasons, older elderly (56%) are more dependent on family than younger elderly (49%). For the dependent elderly, 73% of the cost of an inpatient episode is paid from a family member's Medisave.

To provide a comparative perspective Figure 4 presents the payment shares of hospital bills for the insured (both Medishield and private insurance) versus the uninsured elderly by mode of financing and Figure 5 shows the payment shares of the elderly with and without family support by mode of financing. As expected, the uninsured elderly are far more dependent on their family than the insured elderly (45.4% versus 17.7%). Furthermore, the out-of-pocket component of the payment is almost double for the uninsured compared to the insured. The uninsured elderly also have a larger fraction of their bill paid from their Medisave than the insured elderly. Figure 5 indicates that the elderly who are supported by their children have very little of their own medical savings. Family support itself may be

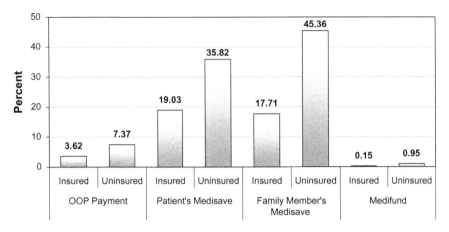

Figure 4: Insured versus uninsured elderly by mode of financing (% of bill paid).
Notes: OOP = out-of-pocket.

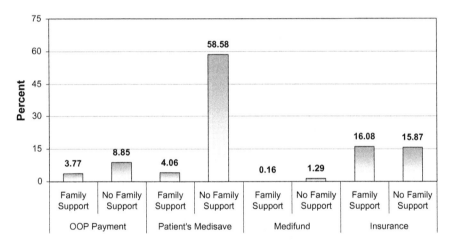

Figure 5: Elderly with and without family support by mode of financing (% of bill paid).
Notes: OOP = out-of-pocket.

an inducement for the elderly not to have much left in medical savings. For the independent elderly, 59% of expenses are paid out from their own Medisave account compared to only 4% for the dependent elderly. Moreover, out-of-pocket payments are higher for the elderly without family support than for the elderly with family support (8.9% versus 3.8%).

EQUITY AND ADEQUACY: SOME GENERAL OBSERVATIONS

The data analysis of the previous section leads to the following observations:

- Government subsidies remain vital to the affordability of basic medical care in Singapore. A majority of admissions are in subsidized wards B2 and C where the average cost is about 20% of the cost in the unsubsidized A ward.
- The present cohort of elderly does not have sufficient balances in Medisave because Medisave was enacted too late for them. The problem of insufficient balances is compounded by their greater draw-down of balances without replenishment.
- The ability to tap on family members' medical savings is very important in paying for healthcare of the elderly. This is an indication of the successful pursuit of the nation's philosophy where both family and the individual are expected to be responsible for the health of the aged.
- Government insurance (Medishield) has a limited value to the elderly as only a small percentage of them are insured. This could be due to the last entry age of 75 years, relatively high premiums and high deductibles for the elderly.
- Private insurance plays an even minor role in financing hospital expenses of the current elderly. Nevertheless, private insurance fairs better than Medishield in covering catastrophic expenditure.
- Insurance cover (both Medishield and private) predicts larger bills. For Medishield, this is to be expected because it is meant for large bills. Further analysis indicates the presence of a self-selection bias in government insurance whereby less healthy people take out the insurance while more healthy people forego insurance and face the risk of catastrophic expenditure. This problem becomes less important as the Medishield cover increases. In the

case of private health insurance moral hazard seems to be the main problem.

- Ward class type shows a systematic pattern of predicting catastrophic expenditure with patients going to A wards facing the highest risk.

- Given that most of the expenditure falls upon the individual and family members, the healthcare financing system is highly income dependent. In the absence of the corresponding income data we cannot say much about the progressivity or regressivity of the healthcare financing system. However, if we take the average monthly household income by type of dwelling from the 2007/08 household expenditure survey[68] and relate them in order to the mean expenditure in Table 3 of the five ward types we get the following hospital expenditure shares of income by ward type: C 47%, B2 34%, B2+ 28%, B1 40%, and A 40%. If these numbers are representative of the actual payment structure, we can observe some regressivity in the payment system despite the presence of subsidies.

Some Recommendations

As noted in the introduction, Singaporeans spend on average only a small proportion of their income on direct healthcare because of the bigger role that indirect healthcare management plays. However, for those who need medical care, Singapore's healthcare financing system is closely linked to individual income levels despite the presence of substantial government subsidies. In an ideal system one could argue that just as the way universal education is provided regardless of income levels, public medical care at the point of delivery should not differentiate individuals by income levels. However, we have to be realistic with regard to the constraints the policy makers face. On the one hand, with the increasing elderly population the government

---

[68] According to the Department of Statistics (2009) these include HDB 1–3 rooms (S$3,091), 4 rooms (S$5,114), 5 rooms and executive (S$8,177), private flats (S$16,311), landed property (S$20,427).

would be strained to finance ever-increasing health subsidies from a shrinking tax base.

On the other hand, financing of healthcare of the current elderly out of children's Medisave has created a rollover effect on future generations and the burden on children's Medisave, especially for low earners, will not disappear soon. Moreover, although many are well covered by employer-paid private insurance, at the moment there is no comprehensive insurance coverage after retirement, the time when good cover is most needed. The Portable Medical Benefit Scheme (PMBS) and Transferable Medical Insurance Scheme (TMIS) are voluntary employer-based and do not apply to retirement. Furthermore, at present Medisave, Medishield and government subsidies are all heavily biased towards inpatient treatment and some cover becomes necessary for expensive outpatient treatment, for example, the newer cancer biologics and cardiology drugs.

Some fine tuning of the current financing system is likely to produce more equitable results with a wider cover without unduly burdening either the government or the patients and their families. One way to do this is to move in the direction of a more comprehensive insurance system without deviating much from the principle of individual responsibility. The government has been fine tuning Medishield over the years and this exercise can go a few steps further. We recommend that Medishield be made compulsory and replace the age-dependent premium structure with an income-dependent premium structure by imposing a Medishield tax, a small fixed percentage of income, with some caps and provisions. Although about 84% of Singapore's resident population was covered by Medishield in 2009, making it compulsory eliminates the adverse selection problem altogether and is needed to implement the Medishield tax. The underlying principle of the tax is cross subsidization from rich to poor, active to inactive, and well to sick. Such cross subsidization, as in education, is essential to provide more equitable healthcare. As Medishield funds build up, the coverage can be increased and eventually it can be made a more comprehensive package. Co-payment and deductibles should be retained to curb over-use (moral hazard) and encourage healthy living. Obviously how to allocate medical expenses among Medisave, employer sponsored insurance and Medishield needs to be worked out. Constant review is needed as the model of healthcare delivery is changing and will continue to change to emphasize more preventive, and more community-based, outpatient healthcare.

END NOTES

Asher, M and A Nandy (2006). Health financing in Singapore: A case for systematic reforms. *International Social Security Review*, 59, 75–92.

Barr, M (2001). Medical savings accounts in Singapore: A critical inquiry. *Journal of Health Politics, Policy and Law*, 26(4), 709–726.

Chia, N C and A Tsui (2005). Medical savings accounts in Singapore: How much is adequate? *Journal of Health Economics*, 25(5), 855–875.

Department of Statistics (2009). *Report on the Household Expenditure Survey 2007/08*, Singapore: Ministry of Trade and Industry.

Eiff, W, T Massaro, Y Voo and R Ziegenbein (2002). Medical savings accounts: A core feature of Singapore's health care system. *European Journal of Health Economics*, 3, 188–195.

Hsiao, W (1995). Medical savings accounts: Lessons from Singapore. *Health Affairs*, 14, 260–267.

Lim, M (2004). Shifting the burden of health care finance: A case study of public-private Partnership in Singapore. *Health Policy*, 69, 83–92.

Massaro, T and Y Wong (1995). Positive experience with medical savings accounts in Singapore. *Health Affairs*, 14(2), 267–271.

Pauly, M (2001). Medical savings accounts in Singapore: What can we know? *Journal of Health Politics, Policy and Law*, 26(4), 727–731.

Phua, K (1991). *Privatization and Restructuring of Health Services in Singapore*. Singapore: Institute of Policy Studies Occasional Paper No. 5.

Phua, K and M Yap (1998). Financing health care in old age: Policy issues and implications in Singapore. *Asian Journal of Political Science*, 6(1), 120–137.

Prescott, N and L Nichols (1997). International comparison of medical savings accounts in choices. In N Prescott (ed), *Financing Health Care and Old Age Security*, Washington, D. C. The World Bank.

Reisman, D (2006). Payment for health in Singapore. *International Journal of Social Economics*, 33(2), 132–159.

Shortt, S (2002). Medical savings accounts in publicly funded health care systems: Enthusiasm versus evidence. *Canadian Medical Association Journal*, 167(2), 159–162.

World Health Organization (2000). *World Health Report 2000*, World Health Organization.

8

MONETARY POLICY IN SINGAPORE AND THE GLOBAL FINANCIAL CRISIS

Chow Hwee Kwan and Peter Wilson

"I'm forever blowing bubbles, pretty bubbles in the air. They rise so high they reach the sky and like my dreams they fade and die." (West Ham United supporters' song)

SINGAPORE'S MONETARY POLICY RESPONSE TO THE FINANCIAL CRISIS

Prior to the crisis the consensus amongst central bankers in advanced economies was that price stability, in the form of low and stable price inflation, was a top priority for monetary policy and could best be achieved by targeting interest rates (usually overnight) or monetary aggregates, such as Narrow Money (M1) and Broad Money (M2). Liquidity in the banking system could be flexibly adjusted on a daily basis through open market operations to increase or decrease the

139

monetary base which would be transmitted to the rest of the economy through financial intermediation. Financial markets would then adjust longer-term interest rates relevant to the real economy, such as mortgage rates and 12-month corporate bond rates, and could largely be left alone to price risk and allocate credit efficiently, since financial markets were generally considered to be rational and efficient.

But there is a problem if banks will not lend because lenders are worried that loans will not be repaid or could not be sold on. The result is a credit crunch reflected in a widening of interest rate spreads as banks borrow cheaply from the central bank but lend to their customers at much higher rates (or not at all) in the inter-bank market. This clogs up the traditional monetary transmission mechanism and eventually spills over into the real economy and produces a deflationary spiral. Monetary policy thus becomes powerless as everyone rushes into cash to fill the holes in their short-term funding and any increase in the monetary base engendered by the central bank ends up mostly in the reserves held by the banks themselves rather than in the money supply. The problem is compounded by the fact that no central bank can reduce nominal interest rates below zero.

Once the global financial crisis had clearly broken in the second half of 2008[69] and it was clear that reducing nominal interest rates and providing more liquidity through traditional channels was insufficient, the emphasis quickly switched to avoiding a loss of confidence in the financial markets, a catastrophic fall in spending and asset prices and a full-blown depression of the 1930s variety. Central banks responded by offering emergency measures in the form of more types of credit, easier borrowing conditions and longer terms for loans. The European Central Bank (ECB), for example, guaranteed unlimited funds for up to six months instead of one week. Meanwhile in the autumn of 2008 the US Federal Reserve (FED) introduced targeted direct lending to the private sector *via* purchases of commercial paper and its Term

---

[69] See Asian Development Bank (2009) and Chapter 2 of this book for the timeline of the crisis.

Asset Backed Securities Loan Facility (TALF), which purchased asset-backed securities collateralized by student loans, credit card loans and loans guaranteed by the Small Business Administration, and the US Government agreed to buy assets and equity from financial institutions through its Troubled Asset Relief Program (TARP).

Moreover, with interest rates close to zero central banks had effectively begun to increase the monetary base through 'quantitative easing' or the monetizing of debt. In the UK the Bank of England bought gilts and corporate debt to increase liquidity and the Bank of Japan purchased medium and long-term government bonds and asset-backed securities and equity and paid for them by 'printing money'.[70] In the US the FED extended its balance-sheet with new assets and liabilities without sterilization. Even the European Central Bank engaged in the practice by increasing the range of assets it was prepared to accept as collateral. More unorthodox measures were introduced where necessary and in many cases governments stepped in to guarantee bank deposits to prevent 'a run on the bank' or the switching of deposits to other countries, such as the Irish Republic, where such guarantees were already in place. In the UK the government took troubled bank Northern Rock into national ownership in February 2008 following a 'run on the bank' in 2007 and acquired a significant stake in other threatened banks, such as the Royal Bank of Scotland. Rescue packages guaranteed potential losses and credit guarantees allowed banks to issue bonds backed by government loans.

In Asia, where the direct financial effects of the global crisis were much less severe, governments tended to respond with more orthodox monetary and fiscal policies (apart from Japan which had been fighting deflation since the early 1990s and whose central bank had been engaged in explicit quantitative easing since 2001), including monetary easing to ensure adequate liquidity and main-

---

[70] Other, more creative methods, used to increase liquidity have included the Bank of Japan's lending of foreign exchange reserves to Japanese companies operating abroad, such as Toyota, and letting small and medium sized enterprises borrow using cuttlefish and sea slugs as collateral.

tain the flow of credit and stimulatory fiscal packages to sustain spending in the economy.

This was also the case in Singapore which, as suggested in Chapter 2, was not significantly affected by the direct financial fallout from the sub prime mortgage crisis and resulting credit crunch. Although Singapore's banks had become more internationalized since the late 1990s and had been active in cross-border mergers and acquisitions in the Asian region, large foreign multinational banks are not dominant in the domestic banking system, so it was easier for Singapore's central bank, the Monetary Authority of Singapore (MAS) to carry out its supervisory functions and ensure a continuation of lending.[71]

Whilst discretionary macroeconomic policies in Singapore are seen to be broadly countercyclical, especially during prolonged downturns, when they can help to cushion the impact and prevent a more severe deterioration in domestic activity than might otherwise be the case, it has long been recognised that the power of such policies is limited by the ultra-openness of the economy. Not only is the Republic particularly exposed to externally-driven demand shocks, but any adjustment through a change in domestic expenditure is weakened by a very high import leakage.

Monetary policy in Singapore since 1981 has been explicitly aimed at providing an environment for sustained non-inflationary economic growth and price stability over the medium-term horizon but, as we shall see, it is also designed to be countercyclical in the shorter run, especially when the economy is overheating and inflationary pressures threaten, as in the second half of 2007. In addition the financial system has, by and large, been well-regulated and a high savings policy has provided a large and growing pool of foreign exchange reserves to reinforce the credibility of exchange rate policy and provide the means for the MAS to actively engage in the foreign exchange market to

---

[71] According to an interview given by the Managing Director of the MAS to the Singapore Straits Times on 10th April 2010, of the 150 foreign banks operating in Singapore none of them suffered a "major incident" during the crisis. AIA, the local subsidiary of the giant insurance company AIG was also largely unaffected despite AIG itself being on the verge of collapse in September 2008.

manage the Singapore dollar on a daily basis. On the other hand, there seems to be a psychological limit to the willingness of the MAS to push the Singapore dollar *substantially* downwards if the economy is moving into a potentially deep recessionary phase, since this conflicts with its overriding mission (as with other central banks) to preserve the purchasing power of the local currency in global markets to safeguard the value of private savings, compulsory Central Provident Funds (CPF) and the official foreign exchange reserves.[72]

Crucial, therefore, to macroeconomic adjustment in Singapore during severe contractions, are complementary policies which can take some of the heat out of exchange rate adjustment. Historically this has been helped by automatic labour market adjustment through a fall in wages, together with direct cost-cutting exercises by the government, including reductions in employer contributions to the CPF and price reductions by the public utilities. In 1998, for example, a package of cost cuts together with improvements in productivity and wage restraint effectively cut unit business costs by an impressive 12% in 1999 compared to the previous year (Peebles and Wilson, 2005).

In the past, there is a case for saying that the main brunt of the burden of adjustment to recessions in Singapore has been borne by domestic workers through wage cuts and cuts to their employers' CPF contributions and by foreign workers on short-term contracts who have been sent home. Interestingly, in the current crisis, although there has undoubtedly been a significant cut in wages and exodus of foreign workers, the impact on Singaporean workers was significantly softened by the Skills Programme for Upgrading and Resilience (SPUR) and the subsidies to employers provided through

---

[72] Moreover, even if the TWS$ were depreciated strongly, the competitive benefits for Singapore's exports would be small while the pass-through of higher import costs into domestic prices and costs would be very strong and quick given Singapore's dependence on imports. All the evidence suggests that it is income effects not price effects which drive Singapore's exports so that the expenditure switching benefits of a large devaluation are small and transitory. The protection of Singapore's savings is part of the implicit social contract between citizens and the government. See Chapter 11 for further details.

the January 2009 S$4.5 billion Jobs Credit Scheme which was designed to keep Singaporeans in employment.[73]

One way to think about this is that during a recessionary phase in the business cycle there is a need to reduce the real effective exchange rate to offset the fall in external demand. This can partially be done by a central-bank induced depreciation of the nominal trade-weighted Singapore dollar (TWS$) but this can be reinforced by a fall in domestic costs. For a historical look at these issues, see Peebles and Wilson (2005).

The difficulties for monetary policy are compounded by the fact that the Singapore government appears to be very reluctant to use fiscal policy automatically as a countercyclical tool in the same way as in other countries, but rather prefers to apply fiscal measures in an *ad hoc* and temporary fashion during downturns. This stems partly from the very large import leakage from a dollar of government spending, but also from a long-term commitment to budget surpluses to support a high savings rate, an ideological aversion to universal welfare payments and the desire to focus fiscal policy on long-run goals, including the attraction of export-oriented mobile foreign capital and social goals, such as increasing the citizen birth rate and reducing traffic congestion.

In the recent economic downturn both monetary and fiscal policies were employed in Singapore to lighten the impact of the global crisis on the domestic economy but the main emphasis was undoubtedly placed on the fiscal response.[74] The FY2009 Budget was brought forward to January and included a S$20.5 billion Resilience Package (about 8% of GDP) to save jobs, enhance the cash flow and the competitiveness of firms, support families, and strengthen the economy's long-term capabilities. A key feature of the package was the S$4.5 billion Jobs Credit Scheme, which provided cash grants to employers to subsidise part of their local wage bill. The government also extended S$5.8 billion in capital for a

---

[73] The adjustment of the labour market during the crisis and the role of government subsidized training schemes is the focus of Chapter 5.

[74] See Chapter 9 for details on Singapore's fiscal policy in relation to the crisis.

Special Risk-Sharing Initiative (SRI) to co-share risks with the banks and stimulate bank lending and ensure that a broader segment of companies had access to credit to sustain their operations. In addition, to reduce the cost burden and ease the cash flow of businesses, a number of tax measures were introduced including a 40% property tax rebate for industrial and commercial properties and a reduction in the corporate income tax rate. To address longer-term structural issues the government pressed ahead with investment in infrastructure, education, healthcare and research and development. These investments stimulate aggregate demand in the short-run but have the added merit that they also produce some longer-term social return.

As far as monetary policy specifically is concerned, the priority in Singapore, as in other countries in the region was to ease monetary policy, increase liquidity and prevent a mass withdrawal of deposits. Bank deposits were fully guaranteed until 2010 and the MAS arranged a US$30 billion foreign exchange swap with the US Federal Reserve (FED) to enable banks to get access to emergency liquidity should it be needed. MAS also loosened monetary policy, but to understand how this was actually implemented, requires some elaboration on Singapore's rather unique exchange rate-centred monetary policy.[75]

Since 1981, Singapore's monetary policy, summarised in the acronym 'BBC' or basket, band and crawl, has been centred on the exchange rate with the primary objective of ensuring domestic price stability as an anchor for macroeconomic stability in general and a sound basis for sustainable economic growth.[76] The exchange rate is monitored and 'managed' against a trade-weighted basket of currencies (TWS$) of Singapore's major trading partners and

---

[75] For the exchange rate aspects of Singapore's monetary policy see Chapter 10.

[76] There is no doubt that, despite its unorthodoxy, monetary policy in Singapore has been very successful since 1981 in helping the economy to adjust to periodic economic shocks. It has delivered a stable currency and low and stable consumer price inflation without sacrificing economic growth and employment, and has avoided balance of payments crises. See Wilson (2002) and Peebles and Wilson (2009).

competitors but is allowed to float within an undisclosed policy band determined by the MAS in order to absorb short-term market volatility. A particular policy band for the TWS$ is identified twice a year in April and October which will ensure price stability over the medium term and the 'monetary policy stance' is communicated to the public in an official Monetary Policy Statement (MPS). This can be fine-tuned if necessary through a 'crawl' mechanism to prevent the TWS$ from becoming misaligned if conditions change in the period before the next policy announcement. The precise width of the policy band and the weights used to calculate the TWS$ are not released to the public but market participants and academics can usually make reasonable guesses about them. This allows the MAS some room to 'surprise' the market on a day-to-day basis to prevent excessive speculation against the Singapore dollar.

Singapore's decision to forego the use of traditional monetary policy instruments, such as interest rates and monetary aggregates, is a consequence of its extreme openness to international trade and capital flows and its desire to 'manage' the currency to some degree. Because Singapore imposes negligible protection against imports from the rest of the world and has little by way of natural resources it must import most of what it needs and export to pay for it. As a result it is a classic price taker in international goods markets and the combined ratio of its exports and imports to GDP — a measure of openness to trade — is in excess of three. What the MAS has done since 1981 has been to turn this import dependence into a virtue by taking advantage of the powerful link between the exchange rate, import prices, and domestic prices. Because domestic prices are largely determined by world prices for a given exchange rate, intervention to appreciate the TWS$ effectively lowers import prices and, subsequently, wholesale and consumer prices, as the effects of the appreciation 'pass-through' to the domestic economy. On the other hand, if inflation is not a threat and there is a risk the economy will slow down or slip into recession, the TWS$ can be depreciated to enhance export competitiveness. Empirical studies have shown that the exchange rate is an effective instrument of monetary policy in Singapore and bears a stable and predictable relationship with price stability as the ultimate target of monetary policy over the medium term. See, for example, the policy simulations carried out in Abeysinghe and Choy (2007).

A second factor determining the choice of monetary policy in Singapore is Singapore's openness to international capital flows. Foreign exchange controls and restrictions on inflows and outflows of capital were resmoved in 1978 and Singapore has always adopted an 'open-arms' approach to foreign investment.[77] There is also a very close relationship between the domestic banking system and the substantially larger offshore Asian Dollar Market or ADM.[78] There is, in essence, almost perfect capital mobility and substitutability between domestic (onshore) and foreign (offshore) financial assets. The consequence of this is that interest rates in Singapore are essentially determined by world money markets.[79] Singapore is, in the financial sense, too small to set its own interest rates in any effective way and the MAS does not seriously attempt to manage interest rates or money aggregates. What it does do, however, is carry out money market operations on a daily basis to ensure that there is sufficient liquidity in the local banking system to satisfy the banks' demand for cash balances to meet their intra-day settlements amongst themselves and with the central bank and to neutralize the effects on the domestic money supply of its own

---

[77] Although there have been some restrictions in place since 1981 to limit the offshore use of the Singapore dollar to prevent speculation.

[78] The ADM is a market where the banks in Singapore which are licensed to deal in the ADM can lend and borrow in a foreign (offshore) currency, usually the US dollar. Even if the transaction is in another currency, such as the yen, it is still referred to by convention as the Asian Dollar Market.

[79] This is reinforced by the well-known 'policy trilemma' which suggests that central banks will have to sacrifice traditional monetary autonomy in terms of targeting domestic interest rates or money aggregates if they wish to 'manage' the currency and keep the capital market open. Because managing the currency is thought to be more effective in Singapore in achieving low and stable inflation than traditional monetary instruments the MAS gives up the latter in favour of an exchange rate centred monetary policy.

foreign exchange operations.[80] Since the money markets continued to operate normally in Singapore there was no need for the MAS to actually provide extra liquidity. In central banking jargon 'no extraordinary measures have been needed'. In any case it could not do so since its money market operations are the endogenous result of its need to keep the TWS$ within its targeted policy band.

Interpreted in this way, Singapore's monetary policy response to the global crisis was to provide any needed liquidity within the TWS$ policy band and to loosen monetary (exchange rate) policy. By the end of 2007 MAS had progressively tightened policy in response to increasing domestic and external inflationary pressures by increasing the slope of the TWS$ policy band (Figure 1) and policy was further

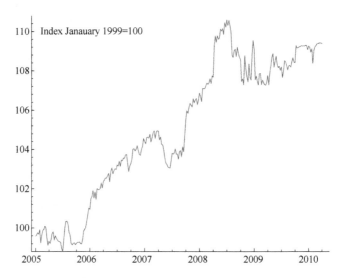

Figure 1:   The Trade-Weighted Singapore dollar 2005–2010.

Source: Monetary Authority of Singapore financial database, mas.gov.sg.

---

[80] For example, when liquidity is drained from the banking system by government budget surpluses or a rise in net contributions to the CPF, MAS may use money market operations, such as open market purchases of government bonds, to inject liquidity back into the money market and keep domestic interest rates stable. Sterilization is not, it seems, an automatic response to neutralize its own forex market operations but depends on the balance of other factors affecting money market liquidity at the time.

tightened in April 2008 by re-centring the policy band upwards to the prevailing level of the TWS\$.[81]

Then in October 2008, against the backdrop of a fragile global economy and dissipating inflationary pressures MAS moved to a neutral stance by flattening the TWS\$ policy band and in April 2009 eased further by re-centring the band downwards to the prevailing level of the TWS\$ but retaining the zero percent appreciation path. In October 2009, with the TWS\$ fluctuating in the upper part of the policy band due to weakness in the US dollar and a surge in capital inflows into the region, the zero percent appreciation was maintained but with no change to the width of the policy band or the level at which it was centred. This was a response to the rebound in the economy in the second and third quarters of 2009.

Finally, in April 2010, and in concert with other central banks in the region, MAS began once again to tighten its monetary policy stance by re-centring the exchange rate policy band to the prevailing level of the TWS\$ and shifting the policy band from a neutral zero percent appreciation back to one of 'a modest and gradual appreciation'. This is predicated on the view that the domestic economy has now rebounded from the downturn and is expected to continue on a firm recovery path. The official growth forecast for 2010 was revised upwards to between 7% and 9% in April 2010 and further in July to a sizzling 13–15%. At the same time, inflationary pressures resulting from rises in global commodity prices as well as some domestically-driven cost pressures are expected to increase in the months ahead as the labour market tightens and liquidity remains high given low global interest rates and a continuing inflow of foreign capital.

---

[81] There was some debate about whether MAS should have tightened further in October 2007 given the sharp rise in inflationary pressures. MAS' own counterfactual simulations suggest, however, that had there been further tightening this would have injected greater volatility into the economy and exacerbated the fall-off in prices when the global economy slowed in the second half of the year, taking into account the long time lags typically associated with the exchange rate pass-through process. Thus, the subsequent decline in economic activity would have necessitated a sharper reversal of policy in October 2008.

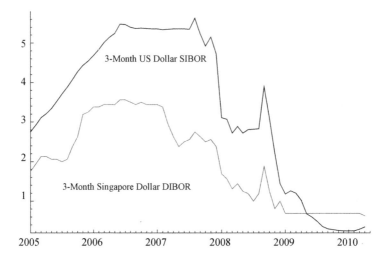

Figure 2:   Interest rates in Singapore 2005–2010.

Source: Monetary Authority of Singapore financial database, mas.gov.sg.

Consumer price inflation is now forecast to come in at around 2.5% to 3.5% this year compared to 0.6% last year.

Figure 2 plots the 3-month Singapore interbank offer rate (SIBOR), which captures global interest rates measured in US dollars, and the 3-month Domestic Interbank Offer Rate (DIBOR) denominated in S$. Figure 3 plots the Domestic Liquidity Indicator (DLI), which is a measure of overall liquidity conditions in Singapore combining changes in the TWS$ and DIBOR. A rise in the index signals a monetary tightening compared to the previous quarter.[82] Liquidity tended to become tighter by the third quarter of 2007 as inflationary pressures increased but interest rates subsequently fell sharply as global rates were pushed down by central banks in response to the credit crisis and monetary conditions in Singapore were broadly accommodative (downward trend in the cumulative DLI) from about August 2008 as the crisis unfolded. Only in mid-2009 did the DLI begin to stabilize.

---

[82] Note that when interest rates are fairly constant, as in 2009 and 2010, the DLI is almost entirely driven by changes in the TWS$.

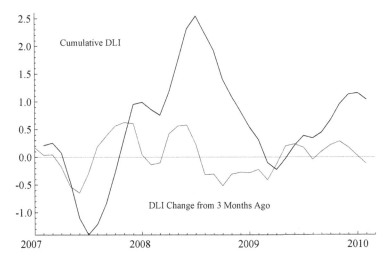

Figure 3:   The Singapore domestic liquidity indicator 2007–2010.
Source: Monetary Authority of Singapore financial database, mas.gov.sg.

Figures 4 and 5 graph the level of domestic credit to the private sector and its growth over time. Credit growth reached a peak in May 2008 and declined thereafter. Despite the fact that the cost of borrowing was falling to low levels, making it cheaper to borrow, the demand for domestic credit in Singapore tends to be more responsive to the overall level of activity in the economy.[83] The financial impact of the crisis on Singapore was thus cushioned by the fact that the fall in domestic non-bank loan growth, which occurred alongside the contraction in overall GDP, was less severe than during the Asian financial crisis of 1997 and the 2001 downturn, due to strong demand for credit in the building and construction industry and from the residential housing sector.[84] As Figure 5 shows, total and business loan growth from the previous year did fall between Q4 2008 and Q3 2009 but consumer loan growth was quite resilient.

---

[83] See Monetary Authority of Singapore (2009).

[84] Based on Monetary Authority of Singapore (2009) estimates, the peak-to-trough decline in domestic banking units' non-bank loans was 0.8% between the third quarter of 2008 and the first quarter of 2009 compared to a 4.0% fall during the previous two recessions.

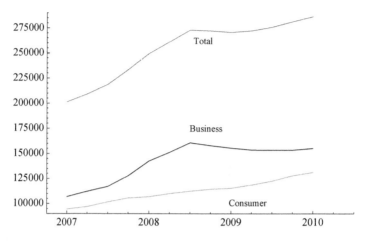

Figure 4: Singapore's bank lending to non-bank customers, S$ million, 2007–2010.

Source: Monetary Authority of Singapore database, mas.gov.sg.

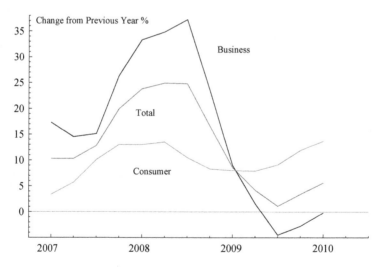

Figure 5: Growth in bank lending to non-bank customers in Singapore 2007–2010.

Source: Monetary Authority of Singapore financial database, www.mas.gov.sg.

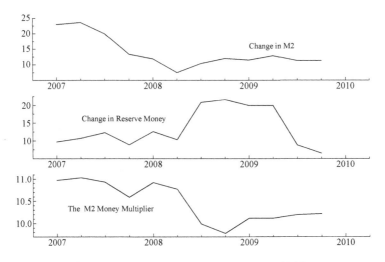

Figure 6: Monetary aggregates 2007–2009.

Source: Monetary Authority of Singapore financial database, mas.gov.sg.

As far as money aggregates are concerned (Figure 6), the broad measure of the money supply (M2), which is determined by both changes in the monetary base (reserve money) and the intermediation of reserve money by the banks through the money multiplier process, fell sharply following the contraction in output in 2008 but stabilized in 2009 as the economy recovered.[85] During the crisis the demand by banks for reserve balances rose as a result of growing liabilities with a spike in September 2008 following the collapse of Lehman Brothers and uncertainty over counterparty credit and illiquidity in international funding markets. At the same time the banks kept higher cash balances as a precautionary measure. Public sector transactions, however, which also affect money market liquidity, were, on balance contractionary, especially at the start of the fiscal year.

---

[85] Broad money in Singapore comprises demand deposits and currency in circulation, together with 'quasi-money' such as fixed savings deposits held in banks plus negotiable certificates of deposit issued by Singapore banks in Singapore dollars. Reserve money is notes and coins held by the public plus banks' vault cash and current accounts with the MAS.

The behaviour of reserve money and broad money is also complicated by net capital inflows from abroad, which increase the
monetary base and tend to appreciate the currency, and the actions of
the MAS to sterilize the liquidity effects of its own foreign exchange
operations on the money market. In 2009, for example, capital
inflows picked up significantly and if MAS intervenes in the forex
market to dampen excessive volatility by selling the Singapore dollar
in exchange for US dollars, this will also increase the monetary base
and may require offsetting sterilization through money market operations. This explains why a capital inflow need not automatically lead
to a corresponding rise in the monetary base and M2 in Figure 6.

Taking all these factors into consideration, the increase in reserve
money (Figure 6) was modest.

In sum, the MAS responded to the crisis by loosening the
monetary policy stance by flattening the exchange rate policy band
and then re-centring it downwards. From the middle of 2008 overall domestic liquidity, as measured by the DLI, trended downwards
as interest rates in Singapore fell in line with a fall in global rates to
low levels as economic activity slackened and central banks eased
monetary policy. At the same time, broad money in Singapore fell
as bank intermediation of reserve money contracted and banks
increased their demand for reserve and settlements balances and
the fall in GDP reduced the number of transactions. To counter
overall contractionary forces operating in the local money market
net of its own foreign exchange operations, MAS carried out
money market operations to ensure sufficient liquidity in the
banking system.

However, monetary policy in Singapore does not work alone.
Indeed fiscal policy has played a larger countercyclical role during this
crisis than in the past and was probably quantitatively more important
than monetary policy. In fiscal year 2009, the government recorded a
primary deficit[86] of about S$4 billion following surpluses of S$3 billion

---

[86] This is defined as operating revenue excluding net investment income or returns
less the sum of operating and development spending. The investment income or
returns are excluded on the grounds that they are volatile.

and S$7 billion in the previous two years. Revenue fell because of a fall in tax receipts while both operating and development expenditure increased. Using the 'Fiscal Impulse' (FI) measure to better capture the overall stance of fiscal policy[87], it clearly switched from being contractionary in 2007 to expansionary mode in 2008 and 2009 (Monetary authority of Singapore, 2010). Moreover, simulations by the Monetary Authority of Singapore (2009) suggest that the measures introduced in the January 2009 budget would add approximately 1.5 percentage points to GDP growth in 2009 and reduce headline inflation by 0.2 percentage points. Monetary policy, by comparison, would have had a smaller impact on GDP growth, although it may have helped to alleviate some of the burden on exporters' revenue streams at a time when they were being hit by falling sales orders.

Overall, therefore, both monetary and fiscal policy switched from being contractionary in 2007 when the economy was operating above potential to expansionary in 2008 and into 2009 when GDP started to fall below potential as the global crisis began to impact the Republic. Although one can always argue that the magnitude of the fiscal and monetary stimuli could have been larger, the fact remains that the economy has recovered much more quickly than expected and the depth of the recession was much less severe than anticipated.

WHITHER MONETARY POLICY AFTER THE CRISIS?

What are the implications of the global financial crisis for the conduct of monetary policy in Singapore?

Clearly Singapore already had in place a number of safeguards to help insulate the domestic financial system from the crisis as it unfolded in the second half of 2008. The ability to access funds from other central banks, such as the FED, if necessary through swap arrangements was one of them. Also helpful was the 'domestic'

---

[87] The FI measure takes into account the effects of the cyclical performance of the economy on the budget.

nature of the banking system in Singapore in which local ownership over key financial institutions is predominant, despite the openness of the Singapore economy to trade and capital flows; and the ability of the MAS to provide funds and effect any necessary restructuring through 'moral suasion' rather than large bailouts or nationalization. Although Singapore had introduced substantial financial reforms in the late 1990s, including the gradual opening up of the local banking system to international participation, a change in emphasis from regulation to supervision in line with the prevailing view that financial markets were generally efficient, and an incremental switch from a rules-based to a risk-management approach, all of which might have increased the risk of contagion from the crisis, in fact Singapore's banks were not heavily exposed to toxic assets and by all accounts had sound financial fundamentals (see Chapter 2).

Nonetheless, some lessons have been learned. For example, the need to tighten supervision over off-balance-sheet activities in the 'shadow' banking system and the marketing and selling of structured investment products. In February 2010 MAS announced new safeguards, including a cooling-off period for structured products and published the findings of an investigation into the sale of structured notes linked to Lehman Brothers.[88] They found some non-compliance with MAS Notices and Guidelines and banned some financial institutions from selling them for periods between six months and two years. MAS also issued a consultation paper to review the 2006 Deposit Insurance Scheme and replace the full guarantee for individual bank deposits introduced during the crisis. The original insurance coverage of S$20,000, funded by banks and insurance companies licensed to accept deposits, will be increased to S$50,000 and the scope of the coverage of the scheme extended to non-bank depositors.

MAS is also responding to regulatory changes arising from the G-20 Finance Ministers and Central Bank Governors Financial Stability Board and Basel Committee on Banking Supervision and International

---

[88] According to the MAS some 80% of investors had recovered at least half of the money invested as of February 2010 (The Straits Times, April 10, 2010).

Accounting Standards Board, which are due to be implemented by the end of 2012. Singapore has formed the Corporate Governance Council to update its standards on compensation and corporate governance for companies listed in the Republic. More regulatory changes are expected.

From a monetary policy perspective, the failure of the traditional reliance on interest rates and money aggregates operating through the financial intermediation of banks was of less relevance to Singapore given its exchange-rate centred monetary policy, but it does emphasise again the limitations of this policy in dealing with a severe downturn in the absence of a strong fiscal stimulus and, if necessary, other unorthodox cost-cutting measures. It also raises an interesting question: if necessary would MAS resort to extensive quantitative easing along the lines of the US and UK if the domestic financial system were on the brink of collapse?

Surprisingly, there are no obvious institutional or psychological constraints to this happening. The MAS is not an independent central bank and there is no historical evidence to suggest that it would be unwilling to cooperate with the Finance Ministry to provide targeted direct lending to the private sector if necessary. Neither is there any reason to believe that it would rule out the 'nuclear option' of 'printing money'. Singapore does not run a currency board system in the same manner as Hong Kong but it does have a Currency Board located within the MAS which, under the Currency Act, must maintain sufficient foreign assets in its Currency Fund to provide 100% backing for any currency notes it issues to the banks.[89]

However, since the Currency Board holds foreign currency reserves well in excess of the amount of currency in circulation, this should not be a binding constraint. Anyway the law could always be changed. Of course, quantitative easing would not be its first choice, given the inflationary risks, but it need not be ruled out. The more subtle problem would be whether the subsequent increase in liquidity

---

[89] For the differences between the currency boards in Singapore and Hong Kong, see Peebles and Wilson (2002).

would depreciate the Singapore dollar to an unacceptable level in terms of its purchasing power in international markets. On the other hand, one of the lessons from the credit crunch is that there may be worse things than inflation, and financial stability, as opposed to price stability, may need to be incorporated more explicitly into the policy objectives of central banks.

Allied to this is the controversial issue whether a central bank should tighten monetary policy preemptively in order to moderate asset price bubbles before a sudden bust triggers financial instability, such as a large rise in non-performing loans?[90]

An asset price bubble is generally characterized as a persistent increase in an asset price that is not fully justified by fundamentals but is caused by speculative activity and occurs mostly in periods of easy credit and high leverage. The buildup in the asset price misalignment implodes at some point, often unexpectedly, with a sharp correction. An extreme case of this is what Noriel Roubini (2005, 2009) has described a 'monster bubble' when cheap credit leads to speculative leveraging in a wide range of risk assets, including commodities. When central banks eventually tighten monetary policy, the unwinding leads to a crash.

On the other hand, if the burst in economic activity is more akin to Mishkin's (2008) 'echo bubble', the situation may be far less serious since it is merely a reaction to a crash caused by loose monetary policy and 'irrational exuberance', such as the 1987 stock market collapse. Since there is no cycle of leveraging against higher and higher asset values, the bubble will eventually peter out and central banks are justified in keeping interest rates low.

Figure 7 depicts the Singapore residential property price index and the share price index from the first quarter of 1985 to the last quarter of 2009. The Singapore housing market experienced several boom-bust cycles during this period, with an average quarter-on-quarter growth of 1.5%. Sharp appreciations in house prices occurred in periods of rapid

---

[90] Much of the discussion here has been taken from Chow and Choy (2009). For more on the debate over the relationship between monetary policy and bubbles, see Bernanke and Gertler (2001), Mishkin (2008), Roubini (2005) and White (2009).

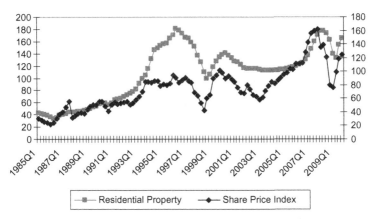

Figure 7: Singapore residential property and stock price indices.
Source: CEIC Database and International Monetary Fund International Financial Statistics.

economic growth and were mostly associated with the liberalization of the housing finance sector and, in particular, CPF regulations. Conversely, downturns in house prices coincided with economic recessions or the implementation of anti-speculation measures such as direct credit controls. The quarter-on-quarter house price inflation rates range from −14.1% to 15.8%, partly reflecting the rise and fall of foreign investor interest in the Singapore property market.

Compared to house prices, stock prices in Singapore have a higher average quarter on-quarter growth rate of 2.3%. As expected, swings in stock price cycles are more pronounced with the growth rates spanning a wider range of −43.1% to 42.8%. The cyclical behavior in stock prices is related to business cycles as well as the ebb and flow of foreign portfolio investment in the local stock market.

Should central banks react to bubbles using the instruments of monetary policy?

One lesson from the present global financial crisis is that policymakers should not practice benign neglect in the face of asset price bubbles. If the bubbles are big enough the result could be inflation and then a fall in economic activity below desired levels which monetary policy may not easily be able to rectify after the fact. Moreover, not leaning against asset prices could be more harmful to the economy because mopping up after the event can be very costly and may give rise to 'moral hazard' and further bubbles if investors believe that the central bank is providing insurance against downside risks. This may then encourage them to take on excessive risks during the upswing, thereby exacerbating the bubble. On the other hand, tightening monetary policy during an upturn would reduce the financial institutions' exposure to bad debts and lessen the severity of subsequent real and financial disruptions. Furthermore, credible statements by the central bank that it is concerned and would be willing to act could move private sector behavior in a more stabilizing direction (White, 2009). While this is unlikely to get rid of the bubble entirely, its size would arguably be smaller and the damaging effects less pronounced.

Secondly, asset inflation may threaten general price stability by over-stimulating consumption and investment spending or raising inflationary expectations. For example, swings in house prices can have potent effects on the economy *via* their impact on household wealth, as the recent collapse in the US housing market has shown, while a stock price boom could be costly to the extent that it encourages excessive business investment in sub-optimal projects. Moreover, if proactive monetary tightening is viewed as an insurance against the risk of economic damage brought on by an eventual crash, then the uncertainty of the boom would still justify preemptive action, just as a homeowner needs to take some fire insurance even though he is uncertain that his house will burn down (Borio and White, 2003).

The case for pro-active policy of some kind is also strengthened if bubbles are seen not as one-off events but rather as a permanent feature of the economic environment. As Singapore's Finance Minister, Tharman Shanmugaratnam puts it:

> "Bubbles occur frequently-more so than can be explained if the 'efficient-market hypothesis' holds. They are prolonged, and can cause considerable economic damage when they burst. Bubbles and the miss-pricing of risk are not exceptional events, but part of the regular functioning of the financial markets."[91]

---

[91] See Shanmugaratnam (2009a).

There is, however, a widespread view prevalent among central bankers themselves, that monetary policy specifically should not react to anticipated bubbles. A key argument is that bubbles are, by definition, extremely difficult to identity and there is a lack of precise criteria for determining if the change in asset prices is consistent with the change in economic fundamentals.[92] How then should the central bank react to a bubble when there is uncertainty about its size and indeed whether it even exists at all? Is it a 'monster' bubble in the making or merely an 'echo' bubble?

A good example of this was at the beginning of 2010 when there were different views as to whether there were bubbles building up in the Beijing, Shanghai and Hong Kong property markets or whether it was the result of genuine demand. In China's case this was compounded by the fact that there was little evidence of bubbles elsewhere in the economy.[93]

This argument is strengthened if there were to be collateral damage from preemptive tightening on other parts of the economy. In other words, there is no 'safe popping' of asset price bubbles since monetary policy is a blunt instrument. Given expectations of further increases in asset prices, the tightening required to quash any market euphoria may have to be severe and hence, might throw the economy into recession. According to this point of view policy makers should be 'clean' rather than 'lean', that is, the central bank should wait for the bubble to collapse and then adopt traditional monetary easing to deal with the aftermath instead of preemptive

---

[92] See the opposing views about China's property bubble in the Singapore Business Times of June 17, 2010.

[93] Since then (May 2010) clearer evidence has emerged that property bubbles are indeed building up in both China and Hong Kong and the authorities have responded accordingly. In Beijing families are now limited to buying one new apartment and cannot receive a loan if they have not paid their taxes or social security contributions and the government is reclaiming land hoarded by developers. In Hong Kong stamp duty has been increased for luxury flats, corporate purchases are now restricted to 10% of total sales and the supply of land has been increased. In August 2010, the rules were tightened further.

tightening during an upswing. After all, accommodative monetary policy after the bust would not only help the financial sector to cope with balance sheet vulnerabilities but will also soften the blow on aggregate demand.

A second argument against using monetary policy to counter potential bubbles is that the central bank already has too many objectives to be achieved with a limited range of policy instruments. Indeed, perhaps monetary policy should serve exclusively as a counter-cyclical tool and asset price fluctuations that do not affect inflation within the central bank's forecast horizon, that is one to two years, should be ignored (Bernanke and Gertler, 2001).

This fits in with those who feel that central banks, especially in emerging economies, already have a difficult job trying to achieve a range of goals simultaneously. For example, by late 2009 foreign funds had begun to flow rapidly into emerging Asia and in a world of mobile short-term capital flows and volatile exchange rate movements threatened to create bubbles in stock and property markets as investors anticipated higher returns than in developed countries where interest rates were historically low. The dilemma is that if Asian central banks respond by forcing up interest rates through tighter monetary policy this would have the perverse effect of attracting even more foreign capital. Moreover, if their currencies are appreciating because of a fall in the US dollar, this puts pressure on their central banks to intervene in the foreign exchange market to offset a potential loss of export competitiveness by selling their own currencies. But this has the effect of further increasing domestic liquidity. There are no easy fixes and adding asset price bubbles into the equation can only make life more difficult for central banks.

Linked to this is the view that using monetary policy to lean against asset prices will complicate central bank communication to the public. In particular, the use of the word "bubble" could lead to misinterpretation and cause asset prices to react in unpredictable ways. For example, tightening of monetary policy by the Bank of China in January 2010 led to a sharp fall in stock prices in Shanghai.

Moreover, monetary policy is not the only policy that can mitigate asset price bubbles. Fiscal and macro-prudential policies might offer better alternatives and monetary policy may not be the most effective or the most precise instrument. For instance, if the surges in asset valuations are confined to particular sectors (or cities) or are the result of productivity improvements, directed prudential policies, such as varying the ceiling in loan-to-value ratios, may be more appropriate.

This seems to be the view of the MAS according to its Managing Director Heng Swee Kiat:

> "In our case because we are also a regulator, we don't think we should use monetary policy in a blunt way. Monetary policy should respond to the real economic conditions going forward. And so we need to keep a very clear focus on using monetary policy to anchor inflation expectations and make sure we don't use it for more than we can deliver."[94]

As well as the Ministry of Finance:

> "The government will respond to the property bubble "in a calibrated fashion to prevent boom and bust in the property market. It won't involve macro levers such as interest rates since they apply across the board to businesses at large not just to asset markets so and risk engendering a slump. So Use credit rules, land supply decisions and, in the extreme, tax policies. It is also difficult to monitor 4–5 years ahead."[95]

In the third quarter of 2009, a 16% surge in property prices in Singapore persuaded the government to release more land for development and disallow borrowers from deferring property payments. In February 2010 further measures were introduced to cool the property market, following a spike in the sales and prices of private new homes in the form of an additional 3% stamp duty if a property is sold within one year of purchase and lending institutions (apart from the Housing Board) were now only allowed to lend up to 80% of the purchase price instead of 90%. By working directly on lending margins and countering speculative purchasing directly there was seen to be no need for aggressive monetary policy, particularly at a time when the economic outlook was still uncertain, as was the case in early 2010.

---

[94] Heng (2009) according to *The Wall Street Journal's* Real Time Blog on October 21, 2009.

[95] Shanmugaratnam (2009b).

Nonetheless, whether monetary policy should be used as a tool for limiting upswings in asset prices in Singapore still depends empirically on the effectiveness of such policy in offsetting asset price movements and, if the answer is yes, what the costs would be if the bubble is deflated at the expense of slower economic growth and higher unemployment. Moreover, since it is the mission of MAS to promote sustained non-inflationary economic growth, it is also important to understand the effects of asset price inflation on consumer price inflation over the medium to long term.

In order to answer these questions empirically Chow and Choy (2009) examined Singapore's monetary system with particular reference to local stock price and house price cycles.[96] GDP and the consumer price index are used to represent domestic economic activity and price movements, while the Singapore residential property price index and the Stock Exchange of Singapore (SES) price index are used to proxy asset prices in the economy. For the reasons given earlier, the TWS$ exchange rate is also included because Singapore is a very small and open economy but, more importantly, because changes in the TWS$ are a key indicator of the monetary policy stance in Singapore. Interest rates and monetary aggregates, on the other hand, are not included since the MAS does not explicitly target these variables when it carries out monetary policy.

The time paths of the variables in the model following a one time shock to monetary policy are then traced out and provide an indicator of the extent to which monetary policy might influence asset prices. At the same time, the responses of inflation and output growth serve as an indication of both the benefits and costs of monetary policy.

---

[96] They utilize a factor augmented VAR (FAVAR) model. The VAR model is a dynamic system of equations that allows for interactions between economic variables while imposing minimal assumptions about the underlying structure of the economy while FAVAR models permit the incorporation of information from large datasets in a parsimonious manner in order to adequately capture the information monitored by the central bank for a better identification of monetary policy innovations. The monetary VAR is augmented in this case with common factors extracted from a large panel dataset spanning 127 local and foreign economic time series from the first quarter of 1980 to the second quarter of 2008.

The results suggest that the growth rates of asset prices in Singapore fall by a much greater extent than the growth rates of output and inflation when there is a contractionary monetary policy shock. This implies that monetary policy might indeed be effective in leaning against upswings in property and stock prices in Singapore. Furthermore, housing asset inflation contributes about 18% to changes in consumer price inflation after 4 years so monetary policy could lean against the build-up of asset price misalignments even if near-term inflation pressures remain relatively subdued.

These results are, of course, preliminary and more work will need to be done to see if there are links in the data through which monetary policy could influence asset prices. The dynamics here are also very difficult to model since monetary policy actions are unlikely to have only temporary effects so a strong monetary policy reaction to a potential asset price bubble may risk having significant collateral damage to GDP growth in the longer period. Also the model does not explicitly take into account the Uncovered Interest Parity or UIP relationship which seems to hold for Singapore empirically and suggests that a strengthening currency to offset a bubble would lead to stronger capital inflows and a further stimulus to asset prices through downward pressure on domestic interest rates. Given the constraints under which the MAS operates, including extreme vulnerability to external shocks and the use of only one effective instrument (the TWS$) to deal with multiple objectives, it is difficult to envisage that it would also want to use monetary policy to address bubbles any time soon. Nonetheless the global financial crisis has made it more likely that central banks, such as the MAS, will have to monitor bubbles more closely than they have done in the past, make policy statements about them beyond Alan Greenspan's famous 'irrational exuberance', and communicate their views to the public.

It may be difficult to identify a bubble but this does not preclude central banks from extracting information provided by asset price developments on the outlook for output and inflation in the medium term and responding to rising asset prices, albeit in a more muted fashion, if they judge that sufficient is known to suggest that prices are moving well beyond what the fundamentals might suggest. For example, given the likely correlation between credit cycles and asset price cycles, monitoring variables, such as 'credit' growth, which may have some causal impact on asset price bubbles can provide a practical way of dealing with the situation and would make communication to the public simpler. On the other hand, monetary policy that acts too narrowly in terms of paying insufficient attention to signs of financial vulnerability may itself encourage the run up in asset prices. In other words, financial stability is ultimately to some degree endogenous to monetary policy.

There is also need for monetary policy to work in tandem with financial policies on macro-prudential regulation and supervision even though the linkages between asset prices, financial instability and monetary policy are complex, if only to reduce the pro-cyclicality of credit cycles in order to combat instabilities caused by asset price bubbles. If the circumstances that call for preemptive monetary restrictions can also be inferred from weaknesses in private sector balance sheets and prevailing market expectations, as well as from movements in macroeconomic variables, such as output growth and headline inflation it follows that there should be coordination between the monetary and prudential authorities. In this way an analysis of monetary conditions and financial flows can provide important complements to the usual macroeconomic models used by central banks. Since supervisory and macro-prudential policies are also the responsibility of MAS, this should be an easier task than in other countries where they have either been divested on the assumption that financial markets are generally efficient, or are located in separate and often competing institutions, as in the UK before the crisis.

END NOTES

Abeysinghe, T and K M Choy (2007). *The Singapore Economy: An Econometric Approach*. London: Routledge.

Asian Development Bank (2009). Enduring the uncertain global environment: Anatomy of a global crisis. *Asian Economic Outlook*. Manila: Asian Development Bank.

Bernanke, B and M Gertler (2001). Should central banks respond to movements in asset prices? *American Economic Review*, 91(2), 253–257.

Borio, C and W White (2003). Whither monetary and financial stability? The implications of evolving policy regimes. In *Monetary Policy and Uncertainty: Adapting to a Changing Economy*, a symposium sponsored by the Federal Reserve Bank of Kansas City, Jackson Hole, Wyoming, 28–30 August.

Chow, H K and K M. Choy (2009). *Monetary Policy and Asset Prices in a Small Open Economy: A Factor-Augmented VAR Analysis for Singapore*. Singapore: Singapore Management University Economics & Statistics, Working Paper Series No. 11–2009.

Heng, S K (2009). The Wall Street Journal's Real Time Blog, October 21.

Mishkin, F (2008). How Should We Respond to Asset Price Bubbles? Speech at the Wharton Financial Institutions Center and Oliver Wyman Institute's Annual Financial Risk Roundtable, Philadelphia, Pennsylvania, May 15.

Monetary Authority of Singapore (2009). *Macroeconomic Review*. Singapore: Monetary Authority of Singapore, October.

Monetary Authority of Singapore (2010). *Macroeconomic Review*. Singapore: Monetary Authority of Singapore, April.

Peebles, G and P Wilson (2002). *Economic Growth and Development in Singapore: Past and Future.* Cheltenham, UK: Edward Elgar Publishing.

Peebles, G and P Wilson (2005). *Don't Frighten the Horses: the Political Economy of Singapore's Foreign Exchange Rate Regime since 1981.* Singapore: Singapore Centre for Applied and Policy Economics (SCAPE), Working Paper 2005/06.

Roubini, N (2005). Why central banks should burst bubbles. *International Finance*, 1(5), 87–107.

Roubini, N (2009). Monster of all carry trades faces an inevitable bust. *Financial Times*, November 1.

Shanmugaratnam, T (2009a). Learning from facts, not beliefs. Singapore: The Straits Times, September 21.

Shanmugaratnam, T (2009b). Singapore: The Straits Times, September 11.

White, W (2009). *Should Monetary Policy Lean or Clean?* Federal Reserve Bank of Dallas Globalization and Monetary Policy Institute, Working Paper No. 34.

Wilson, P (2009). Monetary policy in Singapore: A BBC approach. In Chia Wai Mun and Sng Yui Ying (eds.), *Singapore and Asia in a Globalized World*. Singapore: World Scientific.

Chapter

9

FISCAL POLICY IN SINGAPORE AND THE 2010 BUDGET

Lee Soo Ann

INTRODUCTION

The 2010 Budget is striking in its acknowledgement that the Singapore economy has to be restructured "towards higher-valued activities and exit from less efficient ones".[97] Yet the Budget Statement also acknowledged that "the government cannot decide which enterprises should succeed or phase out... We must rely on the market to achieve this restructuring".

Although the budget was deemed to have a near neutral fiscal impulse[98], it was intended to have a positive productivity impulse on

---

[97] The 2010 Budget Speech is found at http://www.mof.gov.sg/budget_2010. All quotations from the Budget Speech in this chapter are from this source.

[98] The fiscal impulse is defined as the first-order stimulus to aggregate demand arising from fiscal policy during a given period. It focuses on the change in fiscal stance from year to year. In FY (fiscal year) 2009 and FY2008, the fiscal impulse was positive at about 2% and 4% of GDP, respectively, while in FY2007 it was negative at about 2.6%.

the economy over the longer term. The key goal, as stated by the Finance Minister, was to "grow our productivity by 2% to 3% per year over the next decade, more than double the 1% achieved over the last decade". On the one hand, the market will call the shots and yet it is presumed that the government can influence it in the direction of higher productivity. A major instrument of the government is the budget as it accounts for 15% of national economic activity. This is the first time that productivity has been openly acknowledged as the priority goal of national economic policy. In the past economic growth has been the acknowledged as the primary goal from year to year, including recovery from recessions.

The 2009 budget had been focused on recovery from an impending recession through the saving of jobs. The latter was accomplished by a Resilience Package comprising a Jobs Credit Scheme and a Skills Programme for Upgrading and Resilience (SPUR). The former was accomplished by allowing a continued inflow of foreign workers. The Minister admitted that the 8% growth in GDP in 2004 to 2007 was achieved because "companies could obtain the workers they needed to seize opportunities to expand while the environment was favourable". The workforce grew rapidly over those four years by 5% annually with foreigners accounting for about half the growth.

Now, however, with a focus on raising productivity, the supply of foreign workers had to be managed. To quote: "reducing our dependence on foreign workers will pay off in higher productivity over the long term, but there are real trade-offs in growth and incomes over the shorter term". Dependence on foreign workers will be reduced by raising the foreign worker levy. The intention is to keep the figure for foreign workers constant at about 1 million a year. The Minister stated:

> "...if we make low cost foreign workers too readily available, employers will not have sufficient incentive to upgrade their operations and upskill their workers. But if we cut too sharply on the supply of foreign workers, then despite companies' best efforts to raise productivity, they may not be able to compete with other Asian players, and in many industries they will not find enough local workers to grow."

Consequently, the 2010 budget was intended to give strong support for individual industries and enterprises to upgrade:

> "We will give significant tax benefits to businesses that invest in skills and innovation, thereby lowering their effective tax rates. We will also provide grants for customized, industry-based initiatives."

The aggregate of tax benefits and grants constitute a fiscal challenge in view of the restructuring of the economy envisaged in the Report of the Economic Strategies Committee published a month earlier than the release of the budget in March 2010. The ESC stated that skills, innovation and productivity were to be the basis of sustaining the economic growth of Singapore. Furthermore, Singapore must be a vibrant and distinctive global city.[99]

THE 2010 BUDGET

Tax Benefits

The 2010 budget introduced a "Productivity and Innovation Credit" scheme. Tax deductions were provided for investments in a broad range of activities along the innovation value chain. Six activities were identified, namely research and development; registration of intellectual property (including patents, trademarks and designs); acquisition of intellectual property, for example when a company buys a patent or copyright for use in its business; design activities; automation through technology or software and training of employees.

Under this scheme, businesses can deduct 250% of their expenditures on each of these activities from their taxable income, up to S$300,000 for each activity so as to focus the benefits on small and medium enterprises. Giving an example, it was stated that a business can get back one quarter of its investment assuming a marginal tax rate of 17%. As currently only the first category (research and

---

[99] For more details on the recommendations of the ESC, see Chapter 2.

development) qualifies for tax deductions up to 150% of expenditure, the new scheme was expected to spur a broader range of innovative activities.

Grants for Retraining[100]

As for the last category (the training of employees), the Minister introduced a Workfare Training Scheme (WTS) to complement the existing Workfare Income Supplement (WIS) which had been designed to help older low-wage workers to stay in the workforce. The WTS is not only open to all current recipients under the WIS but was also to be made open to younger WIS recipients from age 35 years.[101] Under the WTS, employers will be provided with 90% to 95% funding for absentee payroll and course fee outlays. Furthermore, cash grants will be given to the workers on completion of their training, capped at S$400 a year. The WTS will include a structured training programme for those with very low skills, including those who may be out of a job.

Grants in Lieu of Tax Credits

As small but growing businesses could be cash-constrained, businesses were given the option of converting up to S$300,000 of their Productivity and Innovation Credit a year into a cash grant of up to S$21,000[102]. This was intended to help businesses starting off with low taxable income but want to grow by investing in technology or upgrading their operations.

---

[100] For more details on the vast array of training schemes available in Singapore, see Chapter 5.

[101] The WIS scheme was itself modified in the Budget Statement, with the maximum payout increasing by between S$150 and S$400 and more going to older workers to encourage them to stay in the workforce. The WIS was also extended to workers earning up to S$1,700, up from the current limit of S$1,500. These enhancements would cost S$100 million annually as they benefited 400,000 low wage workers.

[102] The cash grant option in the Productivity and Innovation Credit scheme will be reviewed after three years.

Grants for Setting up New Funds

The biggest new grant in the 2010 budget was in the form of a S$1 billion injection in 2010 into a National Productivity Fund, followed by another S$1 billion, making a total of S$2 billion. A new National Productivity and Continuing Education Council will establish the priorities and programmes of this new fund which will provide grants to help enterprises in all sectors, with special emphasis initially on areas where there is a potential for large gains in productivity. The Fund can also be used to develop centres of expertise for a range of industries, which will grow a knowledge base for enterprises to tap on to develop productivity solutions.[103]

The 2010 budget also stated that around S$250 million out of the first S$1 billion of funding for the National Productivity Fund will be dedicated to raising productivity in the construction sector with three areas singled out: initiatives to help local contractors develop capabilities in areas such as complex civil engineering and building projects, investment in new technologies and upgrading to a higher quality workforce. There will also be a grant of S$1.5 billion for the National Research Fund which had already received S$0.4 billion in 2009.

THE BUDGET IN BASIC DEFICIT

For the second year in a row, the budget would be in deficit (Table 1). The Primary Budget had a deficit of S$5,645 million, and if special transfers are added, the Basic Deficit is increased to S$7,204 million. If we add top-ups to endowment and trust funds, such as the S$1.5 billion to the National Research Fund and S$1 billion to the National Productivity Fund, the overall budget deficit would be S$10,795 million, about 4% of GDP. However Net Investment Returns (NIR) gives a figure of S$7,835 million, therefore making the overall budget deficit S$2,960 million.

---

[103] The productivity initiatives recommended by the Economic Strategies Committee are discussed in Chapter 2.

Table 1:   Singapore's budget Surpluses/Deficits FY2001–FY2010

S$ million

	Operating revenue	Total expenditure	Primary surplus/deficit	Basic surplus/deficit	NII/NIR contribution*
FY 2001	28,496	27,305	1,190	−2,273	+1,375
FY 2002	25,469	27,152	−1,683	−2,885	+3,675
FY 2003	25,315	28,499	−3,184	−3,788	+1,900
FY 2004	27,469	28,957	−1,487	−2,448	+3,043
FY 2005	28,171	28,634	−463	−1,041	+2,777
FY 2006	31,289	29,905	+1,384	−1,238	+2,131
FY 2007	40,375	32,982	+7,393	+6,051	+2,405
FY 2008	41,086	38,091	+2,996	−1,093	+4,343
FY 2009	38,566	42,881	−4,315	−8,500	+7,033
FY 2010	40,726	46,371	−5,645	−7,204	+7,835

Notes: The Primary Surplus/Deficit is operating revenue minus total expenditure; the Basic Surplus/Deficit is the Primary Surplus/Deficit plus Special Transfers (excluding top-ups to endowment and trust funds); Special Transfers are social and financial in nature, such as those given to the poor and the elderly.[104]
* Net Investment Income from FY2001 to FY2008 and Net Investment Returns from 2009 to FY2010.
Source: http://www.mof.gov.sg/budget_2010.

The 2010 budget deficit is consequently about the same as the deficit in the revised 2009 budget i.e., S$2,877 million or 1.1% of GDP. The original 2009 budget had anticipated a basic deficit of S$14.9 billion, but the contraction in the economy turned out to be

---

[104] The basic Surplus/Deficit plus the NII/NIR contribution less top-ups to endowment and trust funds equals the Overall Budget Surplus which is not shown here.

at the top end of the 2.0–5.0% projected at the beginning of that year. The Singapore economy had thus turned out better than expected in 2009 as the Resilience Package, plus stimulus measures by the major industrialized countries, had a positive effect on the economy.

Although some jobs were lost, more job losses occurred amongst foreigners and the workforce as a whole contracted. With an expectation of continued recovery in 2010, the 2010 budget no longer sought to save jobs through the Resilience Package which was to be phased out by mid-year and the budget sought instead to enhance Singapore's growth potential by increasing productivity and enabling local companies to take advantage of the opportunities in the new landscape after the economic crisis.

The main thrusts of the 2010 budget were growing incomes through skills and innovation, growing globally competitive companies and including everyone in growth. To accomplish that, the budget had to be in deficit, even after taking into account Net Investment Income and Net Investment Returns from Singapore's accumulated surpluses. Prior to FY2009, up to 50% of Net Investment Income (NII) was included in the annual budget for spending. With effect from FY2009, however, the framework changed to that of Net Investment Returns (NIR) which is the expected long term real returns on relevant assets as specified in the Constitution. Up to half of NIR could be taken for spending. As can be seen from Table 1, the amounts taken from NIR for FY2009 and FY2010 were much larger than the NII for previous years.

The NII figures tend to be volatile and it was deemed more appropriate to use NIR instead. What this means is that if actual income from overseas assets in any year is below the long term expected real return, actual income in the following years has to compensate for this, otherwise the NIR figure will need to be adjusted downwards. The budget for 2010 put NIR at S$7,835 million, slightly higher than the NIR in the revised FY2009, which was S$7,033 million. If NIR is not taken into account the overall budget deficit for 2010 would be S$10,796 million, or about 4% of GDP, no small fraction as compared to previous years and even decades.

FY2007 was exceptional in that an expected deficit turned out to be a large basic surplus, but all other years in the last decade saw a basic budget deficit. What this means is that fiscal policy is in for a long period of deficits, if grants and tax benefits have to be given continually to drive productivity increases, if not offset by positive NIR. As can be seen from Table 1, the incoming stream of NII from FY2001 to FY2008 was followed by a much higher stream of NIR for FY2009 and FY2010.

As currency is issued by the currency board system, the government has, at present, no automatic recourse to deficit financing from the monetary authority as would be the case in many other countries. The government has in its foreign exchange reserves the equivalent of the natural resources which Singapore is short of, but the government cannot increase this pool of reserves much from year to year if half of the returns from its financial investments has to be allocated to the budget, which seems to be the case for FY2009 and FY2010. The actual wording used is "up to half" but since the base figure is not income but expected returns, it may very well be half or more of actual income earned from the accumulated surpluses of the government. 2009 was generally a bad year for investment in capital markets around the world and actual income may well have been much less than the figure for NIR credited to the FY2010 budget.

FINANCIAL ASSETS OF THE GOVERNMENT AND BUDGET DEFICITS

An interesting page in the 2010 budget reveals the assets and liabilities of the government which in historical accounting (not market value) terms amounted to S$615.8 million as at the end of March 2009. Funds set aside for specific purposes, such as the Development Fund and the Government Securities Fund, totaled S$432.4 million. Presumably these are funds to meet certain obligations and liabilities. Some of these funds are for continued growth and care of the economy through the help it gives to persons, such as the ElderCare Fund, Edusave Endowment Fund and Lifelong Learning Fund. Besides deposit accounts, the other entry on the liabilities side of the government balance sheet is the consolidated fund which, at the end of March 2009, totaled S$178.2 million. It is this which is drawn upon in the budget exercise.

What the earnings are for the assets side of the balance sheet is not shown, but we do know that such investments totaled S$497.6 million, the market value of which is surely far more than that. Of the S$497.6 million, quoted investments are stated as S$237.9 million and unquoted investments are S$179.7 million, all presumably measured at historical cost rather than at current value.

The NIR figures in Table 1 come from such investments. Rather than speculate as to what percentage that is of the market value of quoted and unquoted investments, this page in the budget shows that the government is still able, for many more years or even decades to come, to finance its budget deficit from its financial assets. Nevertheless the shift from the NII framework to the NIR framework may indicate that the returns from portfolio investments abroad are lower than in the past. This means that the budget now needs to be viewed as a medium or long-term annual exercise rather than as an annual one.

As can be seen from Table 1, operating revenue in FY2001 at S$28.5 billion was more than total expenditure of S$27.3 billion. In FY2010, it is the other way around, with total expenditure at S$464 billion being more than operating revenue of S$40.7 million. Such deficits can be expected to continue in the future as expenditure on health care is likely to be significantly higher than at present as the population ages. Defense expenditure may also increase as the government switches to a more capital intensive defense strategy to substitute for a diminishing supply of National Servicemen. In FY2001, defense accounted for S$7.1 billion while in FY2010 it is S$11 billion. Special transfers to the poor and old can also be expected to increase. In FY2001, social transfers came to S$394 million but in FY2010 they were S$1.6 billion.

A large proportion of the present lower income workforce will constitute the group of retired poor in the future. They will have little savings, whether through the Central Provident Fund or voluntary. If they already need assistance now, as through the Workfare Income

Supplement scheme or the proposed complementary Workfare Training Scheme, they will definitely need much more assistance in the future.[105]

Thus far, income tax (both corporate and personal) is by far the most important component of tax revenue which is, in turn, the most important source of government revenue. By 2030, a smaller percentage of the population will be working because the population will be older which means that government revenue as a share of GDP will decline. Tax rates have fallen in order to keep Singapore competitive with competing countries' tax regimes. This could be offset by an increase in the goods and services tax, but this is a sensitive political issue.

MEDIUM-TERM FOCUS OF THE 2010 BUDGET

The FY2010 budget departs from the traditional emphasis on expenditure and revenue (taxation) measures i.e., aggregate demand effects, and emphasizes instead more supply-side initiatives for businesses to operate more efficiently. Incentives to promote investment will lower the relative cost of capital, while policies to reduce the reliance of companies on foreign workers will raise the cost of labour. It is hoped that these measures will encourage producers to re-optimize their capital and labour mix.

A recent Monetary Model of Singapore (MMS) simulation[106] shows that the local unemployment rate steadily declines relative to the baseline before hitting 3.5% in 2012. This means that the potential gains for the local labour force may be limited due to the degree of substitution being constrained by structural rigidities (such as job-worker mismatches) which can be exacerbated by downturns, changes in product lines or changes in job preferences among workers. Thereafter, a tighter local labour market, and consequently higher wages, should encourage firms to pursue productivity-driven growth.

---

[105] This problem is also raised in Chapters 7 and 11.
[106] Monetary Authority of Singapore (2010).

For calendar year 2010, the MMS estimates the fiscal impulse as slightly contractionary at minus 0.1% of GDP. In the first quarter of 2010, the economic recovery caused an upswing in tax revenue, accompanied by the withdrawal of the earlier stimulus measures of the FY2009 Resilience Package. The impact of the policies designed to encourage capital deepening and enhance innovation only become apparent in later years. Only by 2014 will private non-residential investment be higher than the baseline, by 4.6%. By then, labour productivity is forecast to be 1.7% above the baseline of 2010 and is expected to grow by 0.4% on average per year, just reaching the 2–3% productivity growth envisaged by the ESC. In addition, nominal wage increases are expected to outpace consumer price inflation resulting in a real wage increase of almost 2% above the baseline by 2014.

CHALLENGES

Sustaining Productivity Growth

The fiscal policy of tax benefits and grants has to be pursued for the long-term for positive productivity growth to offset the recent trend of very slow productivity growth. This can only mean a continuing fiscal challenge for the government. Reliance on NIR will thus increase. In FY2010 NIR amounted to almost 17% of total budget expenditure, a threefold increase from the 5% in FY2001. In 2000–2009, labour productivity growth was only 1.1% annually. One source of this slow growth was the decline in the incremental capital to output ratio (ICOR) of 0.5% per year. The MMS in projecting average labour productivity growth to be 2–3% for 2010–1019 assumes an increase in ICOR of about 0.2–0.4% annually, a reverse of what happened in the previous decade. This means an increase in the level of investment in the economy.

Increasing Domestic Investment

After about 1983, the Singapore economy ceased to have domestic saving lagging behind domestic investment. In fact the opposite was true with domestic saving now in excess of domestic investment. In the last decade, domestic saving is almost double that of domestic investment. No wonder productivity has been falling! Whatever the capital to output ratio is now for the Singapore economy, an increase in ICOR of 0.2–0.4% annually, as simulated by the MMS, means that there has to be gross domestic capital formation of at least S\$50 to S\$100 billion. The average for 2001–2008 as given in Table 2 and Table 3 is only S\$44 billion annually.

Table 2:   Singapore's gross domestic saving and capital formation 2001–2008

S\$ million

Year	Gross domestic saving	Gross domestic capital formation
2001	66,840	36,852
2002	69,621	32,103
2003	70,709	25,987
2004	87,299	40,344
2005	98,272	40,748
2006	111,263	44,420
2007	131,889	52,195
2008	128,617	79,520

Source: Yearbook of statistics Singapore, 2003 and 2009.

Table 3:   Singapore budget expenditure, investment and GDP 2001–2008

S\$ billion

Year	GDP	Budget exp.	Budget exp. as % of GDP	GDCF	GDCF as % GDP
2001	152	27	*17.7*	37	*24.3*
2002	156	27	*17.3*	32	*20.5*
2003	162	28	*17.3*	26	*16.0*
2004	185	29	*15.7*	40	*21.6*
2005	201	29	*14.4*	41	*20.3*
2006	221	30	*13.6*	44	*19.9*
2007	252	33	*13.0*	52	*20.6*
2008	258	38	*14.7*	79	*30.6*

Source: Table 1 for budget expenditure; Table 2 for GDCF; Table 4 for GDP.

The large amount of saving in the economy is, in turn, due to the low share of wages which is less than 50% of gross national income. Singapore is highly corporatized. Labour is organized not so much by individual trade unions but by the National Trade Union Congress, which is the umbrella body for organized labour. A National Wages Council made up of representatives from organized labour, business and government sets guidelines for wages from year to year. Singapore business itself is dominated by large multinational corporations (MNCs) and gross domestic product (GDP) is often larger than gross national product (GNP) or gross National income (GNI), more so when comparison is made with indigenous GDP which subtracts from GDP the wages and salaries of foreign workers working in Singapore and the profits of foreign companies (Table 4). The production frontier in Singapore seems to have been reached so that domestic saving can only find new frontiers in other countries where labour and land is cheaper. Were it not for factor income from abroad, per capita national income would be much lower than per capita domestic income. As it is, indigenous GNI is only about 70% that of gross domestic product.

Table 4: Singapore's GDP and indigenous GNI 2001–2008

S$ billion

Year	GDP	Foreign Share[1]	Indigenous GDP	Income from Abroad[2]	Indigenous GNI
2001	152	63	89	21	110
2002	156	63	93	20	113
2003	162	65	98	22	120
2004	185	75	110	25	135
2005	201	85	116	33	149
2006	221	100	121	36	157
2007	252	112	140	41	181
2008	258	118	140	42	182

Notes:
[1] Share of resident foreigners and resident foreign companies in GDP.
[2] Net factor receipts of Singaporeans from the rest of the world.
Source: Yearbook of statistics Singapore, 2003 and 2009.

The foreign element in Singapore is apparent not only in its large number of MNCs but also in its reliance on foreign labour, which accounts for about a third of the labour force. The productivity challenge in Singapore is consequently multi-faceted. On the one hand, it is acknowledged that MNCs do bring in new technology which enhances productivity but this depends on what MNCs are producing in Singapore and whether they respond to the tax benefits and tailored infrastructure offered to them. Tax benefits, grants and expenditure on infrastructure deepen the fiscal challenge of raising productivity.

National firms are also offered tax benefits, grants and infrastructure but foreign workers are not targeted for assistance in raising labour productivity, though they can get this through the firms which employ them. It is Singaporeans and Permanent Residents who are eligible for special transfers found in the budget, and for many of the specific productivity schemes. The challenge for the future is that the budget will tend to grow, continue to be in deficit, and will be financed by drawing on past reserves, due to the need to restructure the economy and raise productivity. This fiscal challenge should hopefully bear fruit in capital deepening in the face of rising labour costs so that there will be average labour productivity growth of 2–3% in 2010–2019, assuming total factor productivity growth of around 0.4–0.7% annually over the same time period.[107]

END NOTE

Monetary Authority of Singapore (2010). *Macroeconomic Review*. Singapore: Monetary Authority of Singapore, April.

---

[107] See Table 4 in Monetary Authority of Singapore (2010).

SINGAPORE'S EXCHANGE RATE POLICY: AN EVALUATION

Partha Sen

INTRODUCTION[108]

Macroeconomic policy making is, more than other branches of economics, given to fads and fashions. For instance, money supply targets have been given a quiet burial, inflation targeting has taken over the commanding heights of policy-making without any soul-searching that should accompany such a major shift in thinking, almost a shift in paradigm.

Two ideas have been in fashion in the recent past: exchange rate regimes had to have 'corner solutions' and macroeconomic policy-making should be fully transparent. A corner solution refers to policy-makers choosing either a 'hard peg' — that is a fixed exchange

---

[108] I am grateful to Peter Wilson for help and encouragement when it was needed most. I am grateful to Gaurav Mehta for research assistance and Rajesh Papnai for editorial assistance.

rate system with no discretionary recourse on the part of the central bank to monetize the government budget deficit — or a freely floating exchange rate regime.

Thus if a country wants fixed rates, it must opt for a currency board where its central bank surrenders possible tax from seignorage to those who issue internationally acceptable reserves. It rules out a soft peg, where domestic assets, in addition to foreign assets, also constitute backing for the monetary base. The argument being that an irresponsible central bank would monetize deficits and precipitate an attack on the currency in line with Krugman's (1979) first generation balance of payments crisis models.

The second idea, namely transparency, requires that a minimalist rules-based macroeconomic policy be communicated to the private sector. Crudely put, this says: Why should the central bank with nothing to hide introduce noise into the system? This thinking forms the core of the call for an independent central bank.

We shall see in this chapter that Singapore's monetary policy (since 1981) 'cocks a snook' at both these bits of received conventional wisdom. And since no one can argue that Singapore's macroeconomic policy has been anything but a spectacular success story, we have to ask ourselves how does this unique macroeconomic (primarily monetary) policy work? Can we use macroeconomic theory to understand the functioning of this policy? Or is it the case that Singapore got its bouquet of policies right but we cannot say if it could have done better?

There is quite a substantial literature on Singapore's monetary policy. I shall review this literature and, without apology, borrow from it. In my overall evaluation, I will have a little more to say than these previous studies.

In the next section, the exchange rate-based monetary policy followed by the Monetary Authority of Singapore (MAS) is outlined. This is followed by a discussion of possible theoretical frameworks, including a reaction function and how the MAS has dealt with recessions. We then present the view that the regulatory framework is the important distinguishing feature of policy in Singapore and monetary policy is only a part of it. In a conclusion we consider the issue of transparency.[109]

SINGAPORE'S MONETARY POLICY FRAMEWORK: AN OVERVIEW

Since 1981, Singapore's monetary policy has been based on controlling the exchange rate as the intermediate or operational target. The objective, which is similar to almost all central banks, is to promote price stability to support sustainable economic growth. The MAS encourages the exchange rate to appreciate if the expected inflationary pressures are strong. Recognizing the lags in monetary policy, the MAS acts in a forward-looking manner by taking into account anticipated developments in the domestic economy and those in the rest of the world.

The MAS, as with most central banks, is also the government's banker. In Singapore this involves dealing with the Accountant General's Department (AGD) and the Central Provident Fund (CPF), a compulsory savings scheme. Both the AGD and the CPF tend historically to run surpluses since the budget is usually in surplus and payments into the CPF generally exceed withdrawals because of the present age composition of the Fund.

Targeting of the exchange rate path implies that the MAS cedes control over the interest rate and the money supply. In any case, the interest rate is beyond the MAS' control since it has been well-documented that for Singapore uncovered interest parity holds.[110] But as the central bank presiding over an orderly banking system, the MAS also has to ensure sufficient liquidity in the banking system

---

[109] For more detail on the response of monetary policy in Singapore to the global financial crisis, see Chapter 8.

[110] Ex post, uncovered interest differentials generally lie within the two standard error bounds (with a range of ±2 percentage points), except during the volatile period of the Asian financial crisis.

so as to enable the banks to meet their normal demand for reserves and settlements.[111]

The magnitude of this liquidity requirement can vary significantly from day to day. Since the AGD and the CPF run surpluses, the management of Singapore government securities (SGS) differs from those countries where the government is a net borrower since this provides a liquid asset for the banks' minimum asset requirements while providing a risk-free benchmark for the pricing of other assets. In any case, money market operations — outright sales and repo sales — require SGSs.[112]

The MAS' exchange rate targeting framework has three elements: a basket, band and crawl or a 'BBC' as popularized by John Williamson (1998, 1999). This requires some elaboration.

The Singapore Dollar (S$) is managed against a *basket* of currencies of its major trading partners and competitors — the S$ trade-weighted index (TWS$). The MAS does not reveal the weights used in constructing the index. MAS operates a managed float exchange rate system so the exchange rate is allowed to float within a policy-determined *band*, the level and slope of which are announced periodically (semi-annually) to the public.

The band enables flexibility while allowing the authorities to tackle excess volatility. If the TWS$ approaches or crosses the policy band on either side, or if the MAS perceives that there is excess volatility or speculation, it will intervene using spot or forward foreign exchange transactions. The timing of intervention is at the discretion of the MAS. Usually the exchange rate is set by the market within the band but, on occasions, the MAS may intervene before the band is breached if it believes there is excess volatility or manipulation

---

[111] The money market tools available include foreign exchange swaps, interbank lending/borrowing and sales/purchases or repurchase agreements in government securities. The MAS introduced a Standing Facility — a borrowing/lending facility provided to its appointed Primary Dealers — in June 2006 to counter the increased volatility in interest rates and to complement its money market operations.

[112] A well-developed bond market is also crucial for a well-defined term structure of interest rates and information about the markets' inflation expectations that can be inferred from a yield curve. See Monetary Authority of Singapore (2007).

by speculators. On other occasions, it may allow the TWS$ to breach the band before intervening.

Thus intervention operations may take the form of a purchase of S$ against the US$ to stem the depreciation of the S$, or alternatively a sale of S$ against the US$ to moderate its appreciation. The frequency of these foreign exchange intervention operations is indeterminate, but the MAS will refrain from intervention as far as possible and allow market forces to determine the level of the S$ exchange rate within the TWS$ policy band (Monetary Authority of Singapore, 2007: 13).

Finally, there is the *crawl* mechanism. The MAS periodically reviews the policy band and may allow the band to 'crawl' if exogenous factors at home and abroad so warrant. This ensures that the TWS$ is consistent with market conditions over the medium term.

In implementing this policy the MAS decides on the band using its own econometric model of the Singapore economy, which is not publicly available, with different paths for the relevant exogenous variables, such weighted foreign GDP, import prices and exports. (Wilson, 2008). Note that this procedure is forward-looking and involves a judgment about the most likely path of the world economy with an emphasis on those variables directly impinging on the future time path of the Singapore economy.

The policy is then communicated to the public, principally through a bi-annual Monetary Policy Statement (MPS). Only a forecast path is communicated with neither the weights used in the construction of the TWS$, nor the width of the band. In its MPS in April 2010 MAS shifted from a neutral policy (flat policy band) to a 'modest and gradual appreciation' or positively-sloped appreciation path, which signals a monetary tightening stance. The MAS retains, as suggested above, considerable discretion in the pursuit of its policy. The public can only guess the model behind the announced time path of the currency.

The intervention by the MAS to limit the TWS$ within the band, unless it opts to let the band be breached limits its control over the money supply or the interest rate. However, since the exchange rate is not immutably fixed, the MAS can react in a limited way to money market conditions by meeting the liquidity needs of the banks and the general public. It can conduct open market operations by buying or selling Singapore Government Securities (SGS) in return for cash but because, as suggested earlier, the government and CPF tend to withdraw liquidity from the money market over time, many of these daily money market operations involve injecting liquidity back into the system to keep interest rates stable. Thus, its money market operations are severely limited by the use of the TWS$ as an intermediate instrument of monetary policy and the fact that with an open capital account short-term interest rates cannot move far out of line with those prevailing in the rest of the world. In other words, some sterilization of the money supply is possible to offset its own exchange rate intervention but not very much.

Flexibility about the exchange rate target (whether inside the band, or a crawl in the band itself) means that the MAS is seeking a trade-off between the value of the exchange-rate and sterilizing the money supply, as dictated by the 'impossible trinity'. Readers will recall that the 'impossible trinity' refers to a world where a central bank tries to figure out whether it is possible control the money supply having fixed the exchange rate in a world of perfect asset substitutability, i.e., an open capital account. Given three policy objectives: to keep the capital account open, to manage the exchange rate and to have an independent monetary policy revolving around targets for interest rates or money aggregates, the central bank must choose two and let the third be determined residually. In the case of the MAS, it is not looking to defend a single value of the exchange rate, so it has some control over the money supply. For example, in September 1985, following a speculative attack on the currency, MAS sold foreign exchange but left the effect on the money supply unsterilized. As a consequence the overnight interest rate touched 100% (Monetary Authority of Singapore, 2007: 24).

A POSSIBLE THEORETICAL APPARATUS

How can one understand the exchange rate based monetary policy in operation in Singapore from a theoretical perspective?

The strength of the Singapore model is its flexibility. A fixed exchange rate regime would imply that over the long run, the inflation rate of the economy has to converge to that prevailing in the economies that it trades with. In the adjustment process, since the exchange rate cannot be changed, the entire burden of adjustment must then fall on the goods and labor markets. While Singapore has more flexibility in these markets than most other countries, a fixed exchange rate regime is not a good idea especially when there are large shocks emanating from the rest of the world. Some Latin American economies tried to circumvent these problems by announcing a depreciation path for the exchange rate, the so-called tablita scheme. This does provide some flexibility but it shares with a pegged rate another problem: any fixed rate scheme is vulnerable to an attack because it is a one-way bet against the central bank. A one way bet is if private sector agents believe that the peg is going to collapse, they can attack it by buying foreign exchange. If the peg collapses they make capital gains on their holding of foreign currency. If it survives, they lose very little by buying back at the fixed rate. Fully flexible exchange rates, on the other hand, introduce volatility into the system, especially in a developing economy. Pure noise related volatility could affect real activity — intervention to counteract this would, thus, be desirable. In fact, the TWS$ has been quite stable historically with a standard deviation of 1.47% between the first quarter of 1981 and the second quarter of 2004 compared to 3.44% and 4.60%, respectively, for the trade-weighted US$ and trade-weighted yen, suggesting that exchange rate management has been successful (Monetary Authority of Singapore, 2007).

Can we use macroeconomic theory to understand and evaluate the policies of the MAS over and above the discussion in the preceding paragraphs? I propose three candidate models. But we shall see below that the lack of information about how the authorities think does not allow a formal testing of these models except for the ex post fitting of a reaction function to capture MAS' behavior.

The first and the crudest model is the so-called 'S-S' model. This model is usually applied to monitoring the quantity of a good, say for inventory purposes, or the holding of money balances. There is an upper bound of money balances at which the agent goes and deposits money in the bank, and a lower bound at which the agent sells interest-bearing assets to acquire money. In between these bounds stochastic economic activity determines the level of money balances. Remedial action is taken only when the level of money balances hits either a lower or upper barrier.

While this model is used for the threshold monitoring of the quantity of a variable, it can also be used to monitor the price of a variable. A menu cost argument can make it possible for an agent to be indifferent to changing the price but if the price barriers were breached then some corrective action would take place.[113] Note there has to be some information about the price limits i.e. the upper and lower bounds for private agents to use this model for predictive purposes — something that is not presently available in Singapore.

The second candidate is more promising but also requires more information on the behavior of the MAS than is publicly known. This is the so-called 'target zone' model based on the literature developed to study the European Monetary System before the advent of the Euro, where the member currencies were allowed to float within a band. The prediction of the model, which was unfortunately not quite borne out by facts, was that as the exchange rate approached either of the boundaries of the band, expectations of intervention would make the approach smooth. This was the smooth-pasting condition. The problem with the TWS$ is that the MAS does not announce the band nor, for that matter, is there a binding promise that it will intervene to keep the index within a particular band. This is deliberate to 'keep the market guessing' and leave scope for MAS to intervene to punish speculators.

The third class of model is the 'exchange market pressure' model first proposed by Girton and Roper (1977), and subsequently applied to a number of countries. This is general enough to encompass the exchange rate policy in place in Singapore. This model applies to any

---

[113] See Blanchard and Fischer (1989, Chapter 8) for a macroeconomic example.

economy which does not choose either a rigidly fixed exchange rate with attendant changes in foreign exchange reserves, or a fully floating exchange rate with the exchange rate doing the adjustment instead to resolve 'exchange market pressure'.

The Monetary Policy Reaction Function of the MAS

So the question then is having chosen a managed float how does the MAS decide on when to intervene and when not to intervene? A reaction function of the monetary authority has been constructed and estimated based on the assumptions that Singapore is a small open economy and a true price taker in both the market for its exports and its imports. MAS uses the TWS$ to control inflation since any appreciation of the currency passes through strongly into a reduction in domestic costs and prices. But a nominal appreciation if it results in a real appreciation could harm exports unless there is, as has generally been true for Singapore, productivity growth in the export sector.

$$(\Delta e_t - \bar{\Delta e}) = (1 - \rho)[\beta(\pi_{t+n} - \pi^*) + \gamma x_{t+m}] + \rho(e_{t-1} - \bar{\Delta e}) + \varepsilon_t \quad (1)$$

where e is the exchange rate, π is the inflation rate, x is the deviation of output from trend Δe is the long run change in the exchange rate and ρ is the degree of smoothing.

Khor *et al.* (2007) summarize the estimated reaction function for the MAS as having two ingredients. First the policy is countercyclical since a scatter plot of the year-on-year changes in the TWS$ against the output gap over the period 1980Q1–2004Q3 shows that the exchange rate index is appreciated when output is high.

Second, "the relative size of the CPI inflation and output coefficients suggest that monetary policy has placed a relatively higher degree of importance on maintaining low and stable inflation".

The reaction function is then generalized to show that it is similar to the one for the Greenspan period at the Federal Reserve (Fed). To do this, quantitative estimates of the Singapore reaction function are compared with those of the Fed under Greenspan. Thus

Singapore's exchange rate policy is broadly similar to recent comments by Janet Yellen (Feldstein *et al.*, 2004), which identified several key elements of the US Federal Reserve's monetary policy under the chairmanship of Alan Greenspan. First, she notes the commitment of the Greenspan-era Fed to price stability as a fundamental goal of monetary policy, which has helped to anchor inflationary expectations. Hence, the coefficient on core inflation in Yellen's econometric estimate of the Greenspan reaction function is greater than unity (1.68). This is also borne out in Parrado's analysis using Singapore data, in which the coefficient on inflation (β) is also well in excess of unity (1.89).

Second, the relatively high coefficient on the unemployment gap (1.71) in Yellen's estimated reaction function suggests that, since movements in unemployment commonly lead inflation, the Fed has typically acted preemptively to curb inflation by working actively to stabilize the real economy. This compares with a coefficient of 0.42 on Singapore's output gap (γ), which although lower, is positive and significant. In addition, this coefficient indicates that monetary policy in Singapore is also influenced by deviations of output from its estimated potential level. Third, Yellen notes that the generally predictable and systematic behavior of the Fed's strategy is reflected in the good fit (above 0.8) of her estimated reaction function. The coefficient of determination (R^2) of 0.86 in Parrado's estimates also compares well in this regard.

There are several comments to be made on this. First, with hindsight, the Feldstein *et al.* paper is unwarrantedly hubristic. The Greenspan era has spawned the biggest economic downturn in the OECD countries since the Second World War. But in 2004, when Janet Yellen is describing the reaction function, it seems to imply that the Greenspan years were the golden years of central banking. Second, the USA is a 'continental shelf' and Singapore is a small very open economy. Third, the right hand coefficients may be similar but if the left hand target variable is different, these are elasticities that are different across regressions. The MAS monetary policy surely does not require a certificate from the Fed!

EXCHANGE RATE POLICY IN THE RECENT DOWNTURN

The MAS has allowed a secular appreciation in the trade-weighted S$ since 1981, in both nominal and real terms (Figure 1, Figure 2). This has helped to keep inflation lower than its trading partners. Since 1981 domestic inflation has, on average, been 1.8% while the inflation of a trade-weighted foreign composite CPI was 4.0%. It has however, allowed a real depreciation when it perceives that export competitiveness was hurt, providing this is not at the cost of high inflation. Since it takes 'exchange market pressure' as given, which is equivalent to maintaining an open capital account for Singapore, its ability to generate a depreciation may, in fact, be limited by this pressure.

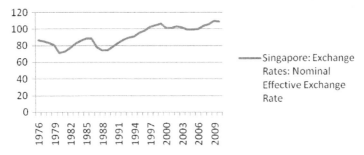

Figure 1: Singapore's nominal effective exchange rate 1976–2009.

Source: International Monetary Fund *International Financial Statistics.*

Singapore experienced its first recession since independence in 1985, caused largely by the deterioration in export competitiveness, a cyclical downturn in electronics, and the collapse of the domestic construction boom. A real depreciation was achieved *via* a reduction in business costs from a cut in employer pension contributions, and a depreciation of the TWS$. The latter depreciated by about 16% during 1985–1988. Following the recovery of the economy fear of renewed inflation prompted the MAS to allow the appreciation

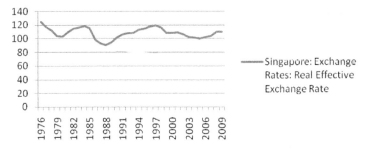

Figure 2: Singapore's real effective exchange rate 1976–2009.

Source: International Monetary Fund *International Financial Statistics.*

of the TWS$ for the next ten years. In the 1990s, real GDP growth averaged almost 8% each year.

In 1997 with the onset of the Asian crisis, the Singapore dollar initially strengthened in effective terms because of the sharp depreciation of the other Asian currencies. As inflation fell and real GDP growth slowed down in Singapore, the MAS ended its decade-long policy of appreciation of the TWS$ and allowed the exchange rate to fluctuate within a zero-appreciation exchange rate band. The MAS also allowed interest rates to fall via money market operations.

In response to the 2001 recession, the MAS reacted by setting the trend rate of depreciation to zero and following the 11th September 2001 terrorist attacks in New York, it allowed a widening of the boundaries of the band around this trend.

The collapse of Singapore's exports, in tandem with the other countries in Asia, in the fourth quarter of 2008 and first quarter of 2009 did not see any major attempt at moving the TWS$ to offset the effect of the crisis. The IMF's equivalent of the TWS$, the Singapore nominal effective exchange rate or NEER, has a value in April 2009 of 109.02 compared to 109.85 a year earlier. The corresponding values for the IMF's real effective exchange rate or REER are 108.36 and 110.51. This would seem to be a very conservative stance given little inflationary pressure. But the foreign exchange market pressure was absorbed by a purchase of foreign exchange

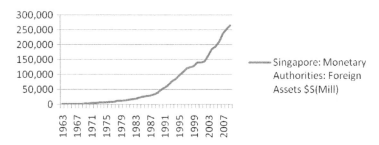

Figure 3: The monetary authority of Singapore's foreign assets 1963–2010.

Source: International Monetary Fund *International Financial Statistics.*

by the MAS since its holding of foreign exchange went up from S$239.8 billion to S$252.4 billion between April 2008 and April 2009 while reserve money went up from S$29.5 billion to S$34.1 billion (Figure 3). Thus, capital inflows may have thwarted a more expansionary stance on the part of the MAS.[114]

MONETARY POLICY OR SOMETHING ELSE

Khor *et al.* (2007) point out some reasons outside the conduct of monetary policy, narrowly defined, which makes the exchange rate based monetary policy in Singapore so successful. In particular, the strength of the real economy, persistent budget surpluses, flexibility in the labour market and long-term productivity growth, takes a lot of the pressure normally facing a central bank off monetary policy. They note, inter alia, that the public sector in Singapore has no foreign debt, while banks and corporations have generally not borrowed from abroad in foreign currencies given the relatively low domestic interest rates. The lack of balance sheet vulnerabilities has also been an important factor in preventing the economy from being pushed into the 'zone of vulnerabilities' and reduced the risks of

---

[114] The amount of exchange market pressure is something missing from the estimated reaction function (1). The more the inflows the more difficult it is for the MAS to achieve an exchange rate target.

intense speculative attacks on the currency in times of regional tur-
moil, market contagion or terms of trade shocks.

Over time the financial markets have become more mature and
better regulatory and supervisory practices have been put in place.
The financial markets in Singapore now have considerable depth and
are able to withstand external shocks with relative ease. The MAS
undertook a strategic review of its financial sector policies in 1997 in
order to keep pace with the rapid changes in global financial markets.
The result was measures to develop the bond market, the asset management industry and the insurance industry, as well as to open up
the domestic banking industry to greater competition. The MAS also
liberalized its policy on the restriction of credit to non-residents in
order to allow foreign investors to issue S$ bonds, and to finance
their S$ investments with domestic funds. (Khor *et al.*, 2007: 22).

Thus with the whole macroeconomic policy framework supporting a well-oiled economy, the role of monetary policy is a supporting
one, though not to be minimized. Singapore has been able to commit credibly to adjusting its monetary policy instruments to limit
exchange rate fluctuations because it has had an impeccably strong
banking and financial system. It has not had a large stock of non-
performing short-term debts in the corporate sector. It has run large
fiscal and current account surpluses since 1989. It holds large reserves
and its combination of strong growth and flexible labor markets
means that monetary policy adjustments designed to stabilize the
exchange rate have not put undue strain on the real economy. Its
political stability means that its commitment to hit those exchange
rate targets has political support and therefore credibility.

CONCLUSION

Monetary policy in Singapore has been very successful by any yard-
stick. It has kept inflation low with hardly any loss in real GDP
growth. Perhaps the supporting factors referred to in the previous
section appear to take some of the credit away from monetary policy
and 'place the crown on some other head'. But it is an incontrovert-
ible fact that the MAS has done a good job of keeping its two ultimate

objectives in good shape while the economy has had to cope with shocks of all kinds and erratic capital flows. Thus exchange rate targeting, unfashionable though it may be, has worked well in practice for Singapore.

As the economy matures, it may be time to reconsider the cloak of secrecy surrounding the formulation and implementation of monetary policy. It is ironic that in Khor *et al.* (2007), while they are comparing the success of Singapore's monetary policy with the UK and the US, perhaps rather mechanically as argued above, they have little to say about the issue of transparency that is a large part of the policy debate. Although MAS has taken some steps in the direction of transparency, mostly to better communicate its policy to the general public and release more historical data about the path of the TWS$, perhaps the time has come when the MAS could share with the public the values of the boundaries of the policy band, and indeed where those values were obtained from, but retain the right to suspend the sharing of information, or indeed, some class of transactions, in abnormal times.

END NOTES

Blanchard, O and S Fischer (1989). *Lectures in Macroeconomic Theory.* Cambridge, MA: MIT Press.

Feldstein, M, M. King and J Yellen (2004). Innovations and issues in monetary policy: A panel discussion. *American Economic Review*, 94, 41–48.

Girton, L and D Roper (1977). A monetary model of exchange market pressure applied to the postwar Canadian experience. *The American Economic Review*, 67, 537–548.

Obstfeld, M and K Froot (1991). Exchange-rate dynamics under stochastic regime shifts: A unified approach. *Journal of International Economics*, 31, 203–230.

Khor, H, J Lee, E Robinson and S Supaat (2007). Managed float exchange rate system: The experience of Singapore. *Singapore Economic Review*, 52, 7–25.

Krugman, P (1979). A model of balance-of-payments crises. *Journal of Money, Credit, and Banking*, 11, 311–325.

Monetary Authority of Singapore (2007). *Monetary Policy Operations in Singapore*. Monetary Management Division, Singapore: Monetary Authority of Singapore.

Parrado, E (2004). *Singapore's Unique Monetary Policy: How Does it Work?* Singapore: Monetary Authority of Singapore, MAS Staff Paper No. 31.

Williamson, J (1998). Crawling bands or monitoring bands: How to manage exchange rates in a world of capital mobility. *International Finance*, 1(1), 1–23.

Wilson, P (2008). Monetary policy in Singapore: A BBC approach. In Chia Wai Mun and Sng Hui Ying (eds.), *Singapore and Asia in a Globalized World*. Singapore: World Scientific.

CITIZEN-GOVERNMENT PARTNERSHIP FOR SOCIAL EQUITY: HOW IT STRENGTHENED WITH THE GLOBAL CRISIS

Chew Soon Beng and Rosalind Chew

INTRODUCTION

This chapter looks at how Singapore provides for social equity through a hybrid of individual incentives and government involvement. The individual responsibility approach requires each citizen to work and save to purchase four basic goods: a house, healthcare insurance for the family, children's education and a pension or annuity for old age. However, this individual responsibility approach is not sufficient to ensure that the average citizen can afford to achieve all these objectives because employment may not be sustainable and the purchasing power of savings may be eroded by the rising prices of these four goods. Hence, the role of the government is to ensure a situation in which there will be plenty of job opportunities and the purchasing power of savings is also protected. The aim of this chapter is to show that this partnership was, in fact, strengthened during the Global Crisis when, among other things, the Singapore government used past reserves to protect jobs.

A SUSTAINABLE SOCIAL CONTRACT

The rights of every citizen must include the ability to get a job at a wage with which the bread winner can afford to buy a house, pay for healthcare expenses for his family, pay for his children's education and have sufficient savings to finance old age living. These are achievable basic objectives if the government and citizens cooperate in a sustainable social contract. If these four basic objectives are part of a government's responsibilities then, unless a country is well endowed with resources such as gold or oil on a long-term basis, it will experience ever-increasing budget deficits, which is not sustainable.

Governments in many developed countries have social programmes aimed at achieving these basic objectives, such as unemployment benefit for people who have lost their jobs. There are also generous pension schemes where employees can retire in comfort. However, this model of a government that provides so much for its citizens has proven to be economically unviable because it creates a disincentive to work. Many Western governments now want to change this model to one which relies more on individual responsibility, for instance, by reforming their pension schemes from defined benefits to defined contribution because the current pay-as-you-earn scheme is not feasible (Gillion *et al.*, 2000). This is not so much a question of population ageing as of bad economics (Feldstein, 1996) because there is cross-subsidization and the ratio of free riders to the hard-working population will increase over time, contributing to the collapse of pension schemes related to old age and healthcare financing, etc.

INDIVIDUAL RESPONSIBILITY VERSUS GOVERNMENT RESPONSIBILITY

What does it entail if we argue that these four basic objectives are individual responsibilities? The individual responsibility approach means that each young citizen has to work to support himself. If he does not work, he will have no income as there is no unemployment benefits scheme to support him. If he works, he will have an income and will be required to save for his house, his healthcare expenditure, his children's education and his retirement.

The pitfall of the individual responsibility approach is that employment may not be stable and wages may not be sufficient. There may not be any saving for many workers and even for those workers who manage to save, the purchasing power of their savings may be too low. Housing may be beyond the ordinary worker's afford-ability, healthcare costs may be too high, poor families may not be able to send children to school and if the inflation rate is high retirees will not be able to cope with the high cost of living even if they have savings.

If the government is not involved or is incompetent, the number of destitute will rise and many citizens will be poor. Relying solely on individual responsibility to achieve these basic objectives for the majority of citizens is therefore not workable.

A government can step in to try to help citizens to achieve these basic objectives. If it does so in a generous manner in terms of removing individual responsibility, employment opportunities may be limited and public social spending will increase. If the government tries to contain the increase in social spending the quality of schools and hospitals will be poor, unemployment benefits will not be sufficient, and the number of poor people will increase. Furthermore, the government will face rising fiscal deficits and a falling value of the national currency. In trying to solve these issues, income tax and other government charges will be raised, which will adversely affect the business climate, and consequently employment opportunities will fall further. This is a vicious cycle.

CITIZEN-GOVERNMENT PARTNERSHIP

The individual responsibility approach may not survive the free market economy, and the government responsibility approach may not be sustainable. We propose that a pro-active citizen-government partnership can provide a sustainable approach to the fulfillment of the four basic objectives. The rationalization is that the government would spend less on social welfare. At the same time, tax revenue would increase as most people have to find work or starve. The incentive to work would help to attract foreign investment. This individual responsibility approach can, therefore, enable the government to achieve a budget surplus each year which could be invested in education and productive investment. Moreover, the favourable fiscal position would enable the government to subsidize housing, healthcare and transport for the poor. Because there would be a current account surplus over time, the foreign exchange reserves of the country would increase. The national currency can therefore strengthen and this would protect the purchasing power of citizens by keeping inflation low. In the case of workers who have difficulty earning sufficient wages due to globalization and competition from foreign workers, the government could use wage subsidies and provide training programmes for them to upgrade their skills. For those who cannot work due to disability, the government could use the help of charities and welfare programmes to jointly look after this group of citizens who are not employable.

Such a citizen-government partnership requires precision in the design and implementation of public policy to ensure that only those who need financial help will get government assistance. Those who can work must be induced to work. Those who need training to find work or to keep their jobs will be given training. Singapore has achieved such a pro-active citizen-government partnership for ensuring the fulfillment of the four social objectives through the following of measures.

Singapore's Wage System

From the 1960s to the 1980s, most workers in Singapore were employed under the seniority-based wage system, by which wages would rise as seniority increases. Only a few large firms employed workers under the pension scheme by which workers would be entitled to a monthly pension upon retirement. The pension payments included a free or heavily subsidized medical package for the workers themselves and sometimes their spouses as well. It became clear that the pension system was not sustainable in the private sector and was soon abandoned. Since 1988, the Singapore government has been promoting the flexible wage system as a replacement as it gives greater incentive for workers to work harder (Chew and Chew, 2005).

In the early years of Singapore's history, Singapore civil servants were also employed under a pension scheme but starting in the 1970s it was gradually terminated as it became clear that it was not sustainable because it was difficult even for the government to factor in the increase in the cost of the pension due to the increase in life expectancy and rising medical costs which would have inevitably increased government expenditure and would also increase wages in the private sector through the competition for skills, making it less competitive globally.

A pension scheme is by far the best system of remuneration for ensuring that all citizens would have sufficient income for old age expenditures but it is not sustainable in Singapore or in other countries. As will be shown later, the Singapore government has managed to convert individual compulsory savings into an annuity scheme, thereby making accessible to most citizens a stream of income from the age of 65 until death.

Singapore's Social Security Policy of Self-Reliance

Since independence in 1965, Singapore has emphasized self-reliance as a strategy for development at the individual and the national level (Lim, 2009). For example, Singapore did not need to borrow funds from the World Bank to start her industrialization programme in the early 1960s. Indeed, the principle of self-reliance has been impressed on every citizen. Singaporeans have been told time and time again that home ownership, retirement and healthcare are all the responsibility of the individual. What the Singapore government is responsible for, and has done, is to make jobs available and to implement compulsory savings via the Central Provident Fund (CPF) scheme.

The CPF was set up in 1955 as the main social security scheme for people in retirement in Singapore (Chew and Chew, 2008) and is a compulsory saving scheme required by law for all working Singaporeans. An employee with a monthly pay of, for example, S$1000, is required to contribute a certain percentage, say 20%, towards his CPF account. At the same time, his employer is required to contribute a certain percentage, say 20%, of the worker's pay towards the same account for the worker. The cost of employing this worker in this example therefore amounts to S$1,200 and is affected by the employer's CPF contribution rate. Consequently, a wage ceiling was put in place to limit the amount of employer CPF contributions set at S$6,000 in the 1980s and 1990s, but the present wage ceiling is only S$4,500 and the present employer CPF contribution rate is only 15.5%. The money in the CPF account cannot be withdrawn until a worker is aged 55 subject to the minimum sum scheme.

The CPF scheme has evolved into a scheme for many purposes (Chew and Chew, 2008). Currently, about 67% of a worker's monthly CPF money is deposited in the Ordinary Account which can be used to finance a housing mortgage while 15% is deposited into the Special Account for old age, and 18% is deposited into the Medisave Account to meet any costs of hospitalization. There is very little social welfare for the young and able-bodied. But those who work continuously can have a house bought and paid for, some money saved for retirement, and would be able to pay for hospitalization for themselves, their children and their parents. It should be noted that a CPF member is not allowed to reduce the total value of his CPF balances except for the payment of medical expenses. If he were to use his CPF for the purchase of stocks or properties, he is required to return to his account an amount equal to that which he withdrew should he sell his stocks or properties, regardless of whether he made a gain or loss if he is under the age of 55 at the time of the sale. Another aspect which is worth noting is that CPF members are not allowed to withdraw their CPF savings before the age of 55, even if they are unemployed. No exception has been made so far since 1959.

However, the CPF scheme is not as restrictive as it appears to be. Singaporeans at any time can use their CPF savings to invest in houses, buy shares and gold and to pay for hospitalization and for their children's education at local universities. These are the investment plans and expenditures any Singaporean parents might want to undertake even if there were no CPF scheme. The scheme merely makes them more financially disciplined. In addition, if members leave their money with the CPF and do not invest these monies on their own, the CPF will use these balances to buy Singapore government bonds. The Singapore government in turn guarantees a rate of return of 2.5% for the balance in the Ordinary Account and 4.0% for Special and Medisave Accounts. These rates of return are guaranteed and are higher than the rates of interest offered on commercial bank deposits. If the government has a large budget surplus, which it often does, it can and does increase the rate of return by one more percentage point. During the current global recession, CPF members have not suffered any loss in their CPF accounts as the government continues to pay the pledged rate of return. In many countries, including the USA, people lost money from financial products and in some cases even their bank deposits. Consequently, the demand for US government bonds has increased, causing the rate of return to fall. CPF members have not suffered such an outcome. The CPF scheme has therefore proved to be a secure and fully funded scheme. There is no cross subsidy between CPF members but only from the government to CPF members themselves.

CPF SAVINGS FOR OLD AGE

Since the early 1980s, the government has become aware that some Singaporeans have not been able to effectively manage their CPF savings when they withdraw them upon reaching the age of 55. Consequently, they found that their lifetime savings could not last long enough. This causes hardship at the family level. Meanwhile, life expectancy has increased. Hence, to ensure that CPF members would have enough money to cope, it was decided in 1987 that CPF members would be required to retain a minimum sum of S$30,000 when they withdraw their monies at the age of 55. They could use this minimum sum to buy a life annuity from a participating insurance company under which they would be paid a monthly income from age 62 until death or deposit the money with a participating bank which would yield an interest, and the bank would pay the members a monthly income until the minimum sum is exhausted; or they could continue to let the CPF manage the minimum sum with a guaranteed return of 4%. The CPF again would pay the member a monthly income until the minimum sum is exhausted. Singaporeans do not like the idea of the annuity as they feel that they would be short-changed upon early death. Hence, most people have chosen the CPF option.

Because of the fear that many people may outlive their CPF savings, the National Longevity Insurance Committee, NLIC, was formed in September 2007 to study the best way to provide CPF members will an affordable, flexible and fair means to ensure that they would have an income for life. The NLIC's report has been accepted by the Government and shared its recommendations at a press conference on 12 February 2008. Hence, in June 2009, the minimum sum was raised to S$117,000 and the government has announced the introduction of a compulsory annuity scheme, effective in 2013 that will provide elderly Singaporeans with a regular income for as long as they live.[115] In early 2010, the minimum sum was raised to S$123,000.[116]

---

[115] For details of the annuity scheme, see http://mycpf.cpf.gov.sg/Members/Gen-Info/CPF_LIFE/NLIC.htm.

[116] Beginning in 2013, citizens born in 1958 and later will have to choose one of four plans provided they have S$40,000 or more in their CPF accounts at the age of 55: LIFE Income Plan — receive a monthly income of S$640–S$700 from age 65 with no refund; LIFE Plus Plan — receive a monthly income of S$600–S$660 from age 65 with a refund of S$38,000–S$42,000 to beneficiaries; LIFE Balanced Plan — receive monthly income of S$570–S$620 from age 65 with a refund of S$76,000–S$79,000 to beneficiaries; LIFE Basic Plan — receive monthly income of S$530–S$580 from age 65 with a refund of S$89,000–S$94,000 to beneficiaries.

The CPF system has a number of advantages. To begin with the four basic objectives are met because Singaporeans are forced to work and save to meet these objectives. As will be shown later, the purchasing power of CPF savings is effective in meeting these objectives. Many Commonwealth countries also have a similar CPF scheme but their leaders have come to Singapore to understand why the CPF scheme works well in Singapore but not in their countries. China, too, has adopted a CPF scheme for housing for her big cities but many young couples find housing unaffordable nevertheless. The reason lies in the purchasing power of saving. This is the reason why the Citizen-Government Partnership is mooted in this chapter.

Home ownership is more than 90% in Singapore. Indeed Singaporeans are known to be asset rich and cash poor. This is because, when they retire, they often have assets in properties and shares but have little cash in their bank accounts. However this is acceptable from the perspective of financial planning as the prices of assets increase over time in Singapore. Many Singaporeans rely on rental income instead of annuity income in their retirement. Those who are less fortunate have to sell their houses upon retirement or mortgage their homes to banks for a steady stream of income till death. As CPF saving is based on labour income, members are also encouraged to use their CPF savings to buy mortgage insurance, life insurance and health insurance which can also help meet some of the objectives (Chan, 2001; Chan and Wong, 1998; Chia and Tsui, 2003; and Reisman, 2007).

As the CPF scheme is based on employment, there is an incentive to work hard and the hardworking population makes it easy to attract foreign investment which will generate jobs for all. The government has been able to use the budget surplus for investment to make the Singapore economy more competitive and accumulate foreign reserves every year since 1965. Consequently, the Singapore dollar is strong and this has contributed to keeping the inflation rate low in Singapore. The CPF scheme has also been used as a macro-economic instrument to reduce labour costs in the 1985, 1997 and 2001 recessions to maintain a stable employment level (Chew and Chew, 2008).

However, the CPF saving scheme also has some weaknesses. It is both a saving scheme and an investment scheme. If CPF members lose money through the investment of CPF savings in properties, shares and gold, their quality of life during old age will suffer. Some CPF members went bankrupt because they speculated on property and shares although this is no fault of the scheme as without it they would suffer the same fate. However, some people have argued that the scheme should be strictly for saving and not for investment, and hence we do not need so much CPF savings.

Those who are physically weak or handicapped will earn less and therefore have lower CPF savings. At the same time, they will use more of their CPF savings for healthcare expenditures. Indeed, some Singaporeans do run out of CPF savings before they even reach the age of 55 for this reason.[117] Unless they have other unrecorded (or illegal) sources of income, the individual responsibility approach does not provide them with a strong enough safety net. Although filial piety is promoted, the government will ultimately have to look after this segment of the population. This is where the government needs to step in and demonstrate the essence of the citizen-government partnership scheme. It is worth reiterating that the CPF Board is about self-financing, and does not require any explicit subsidy from the government.[118]

THE ROLE OF THE GOVERNMENT IN THE SOCIAL EQUITY PARTNERSHIP

To implement the individual responsibility approach as the main form of social security is not easy because it requires political support and it

---

[117] For instance, in 2009, 1,249 CPF members between the ages of 50 to 54 and 7,317 CPF members aged above 55 contributed less than S$5,000 to the CPF scheme during their entire working life.

[118] In 2009, the CPF board had an income of S$628.9 billion. Investment income from the purchase of Singapore government bonds with CPF balances, which is guaranteed by the government, was almost S$620 billion. Rental income was S$23 million, service income was 41 million and interest income was S$140 million. In the same year, CPF incurred S$630.9 in expenditure, out of which S$87 million was employee payroll.

might not be popular. There must also be plenty of employment opportunities available and cyclical unemployment must be minimized or workers who could not find work would be unable to call on their CPF savings for daily support. The government would have to protect the purchasing power of savings against inflation or currency depreciation and set aside sufficient fiscal resources to look after those who fail to make it in the individual responsibility approach without encouraging free riders.

A citizen-government partnership calls for a responsible government. One of the necessary attributes of a responsible government is that it must have a budget surplus and is able to accumulate foreign reserves. The Singapore government fulfills these requirements. Despite being a small and open economy, Singapore has enjoyed low inflation, a currency which has steadily appreciated since 1970 against the US dollar, high GDP growth rates and low unemployment. In 2009, there were slightly more than one million foreigners working in Singapore, of whom 170,000 were foreign domestic helpers. The number of foreign professionals working in Singapore in 2009 was about 150,000. With a 1.7 million active local workers currently contributing to CPF scheme, Singapore is said to be operating at full employment. The ratio of national savings to GDP has been high but fluctuated because the employer's CPF contribution rate has been reduced to save jobs in 1986, 1999 and 2003.

Consequently, the government has enjoyed substantial budget surpluses over the years and these were less affected during the recession years because of a reduction in the employer's CPF contribution rate. Singapore workers did not complain much about this because the recovery from recession was very fast. The use of the CPF as a macroeconomic instrument has therefore enabled the government to continue to build up the national reserves and foreign exchange reserves and provided the financial resources to support a strong currency which has kept inflation low and the purchasing power of CPF savings intact.

In the following paragraphs, we will consider how the government uses part of its expenditure to ensure that housing, healthcare and education are affordable and also to look after the welfare of poor Singaporeans.

Home Ownership[119]

The Singapore government builds and sells public housing to its citizens in the form of Housing Development Board (HDB) units. As the government is the property developer, HDB prices are fixed at about 2.5 to 4 times the annual family income for low-income Singaporeans. For instance, the average price of a four-room flat was 2.2 times the annual family income in 1982. Although the ratio was 4.4 in 2010, it is still affordable. The government has kept its promise because Singaporeans could buy these flats from the HDB and if sold in the open markets after the required five years, the price would have doubled. It is a government subsidy that has preserved the purchasing power of CPF saving in acquiring a flat.

Education for All Citizens

Education is the main avenue for moving up the social ladder in Singapore and there is a close correlation between educational attainment and income level. Those who need government assistance during old age are typically those without much education. Hence, the individual responsibility approach implies that education has to be effective in raising income and must be made accessible to low-income households. Education in Singapore is highly subsidized and there are now four publicly funded universities in Singapore. On average, the Singapore government contributed about S$20,284 per university student per year in 2008, while the average university tuition borne by each student was only S$7,000 per year. All students gaining university admission are entitled to take a low interest rate loan for up to 80% of the university tuition per year.

To ensure that children from low income families do not lose out in education, the government in 1993 started the Edusave Scheme which rewards students who make good progress in their academic and non-academic work with funds to pay for enrichment programmes or to purchase additional resources. In other words, each school student has an individual Edusave account with a certain amount of money from the

---

[119] For some background on this issue, see Lim Chong Yah (1988).

government each year. The balance in the account earns a CPF rate of interest and follows the student as he progresses in his studies until he finishes pre-university education or leaves school. The Edusave Endowment Fund is built up through Government contributions. It is invested and the interest earned is used to finance the contributions, grants and awards given to schools and students. The Government contributed an initial capital sum of S$1 billion to the fund in 1993 and the capital sum reached the target of S$5 billion in August 1997.

Affordable Healthcare

Generally, an employee's healthcare and that of his family are looked after by his employer in Singapore. Hence, affordable healthcare is an acute problem for people who retire or do not have an employer. Within the CPF framework, each Singaporean worker has a Medisave account to buy healthcare insurance. But as pointed out earlier, there are Singaporeans who do not have sufficient money in their CPF account. Hence the so-called 3-M approach to help poor Singaporeans: Medisave (see above), Medishield, which is basically an insurance healthcare scheme for low-income Singaporeans; and Medifund, which is an endowment fund set up by the Government to help needy Singaporeans who are unable to pay for their medical expenses and acts as a safety net for those who cannot afford the subsidised bill charges despite their Medisave and Medishield coverage.

In June 2009, the government mooted the so-called 3-E approach to look after the healthcare of the elderly poor. Eldersave is the setting aside of CPF money for old-age healthcare needs, Eldershield is an insurance scheme for severe disability and Elderfund is a scheme into which the government injects funds to help the elderly poor pay their hospital bills. But the 3-E approach will not be operational for another 10 years or so.

In the meantime, the government continues to provide financial assistance in the form of subsidies to the elderly poor for healthcare. To ensure that the subsidy goes to those who need it, an income assessment framework, called the 'Means Test' was introduced in 2000. In national hospitals, those who are considered poor will only pay S$23 a night when the cost of a hospital bed per night is S$115 in the lowest category of hospital wards. The difference is paid for by the government. The subsidy per bed decreases for more expensive hospital wards. This subsidy is not limited to the elderly. There are poor people who cannot afford to pay for hospitalization who are given waivers after stringent scrutiny.

Affordable Public Transport

Public transport has to be cheap enough so that low-income households can afford to commute to work regardless of employment location. In Singapore bus services and MRT (mass rapid transport) operators are publically-listed companies so bus and MRT fares are market-determined and require no subsidies from the government, which is not the case in many countries. However, the government and the public transport operators join hands to provide transport vouchers to lower the bus fares and MRT fares for low-income Singaporeans. For instance, in 2007, a total of 5.3 million worth of transport vouchers were given out. The government only subsidizes public transport for the poor, not for all citizens.

Market-based Training Schemes

The Skills Development Fund (SDF) is funded by a levy on employees' payrolls. All employers are encouraged to apply to the SDF for subsidies for training of their workers, normally ranging from 30% to 70% of the cost of training. In 2008, more than 400,000 local workers received training sponsored by the SDF. It goes without saying that a web of effective national training schemes, of which the SDF is the main pillar, becomes one of the pre-conditions for the individual responsibility approach to work as Singapore's workforce is retrained every four to five years.

Policies to Help the Needy Elderly

Those elderly poor who cannot fend for themselves and do not have support from their children receive monthly public assistance of about S$300. In 2010, about 3,000 elderly poor received such assistance. About 1,000 elderly poor live in government-run homes. Singapore's social welfare system revolves around charity organizations. In other words, the government promotes and regulates charities for the purpose of providing welfare for the poor and the elderly. There are almost 5000 elderly staying in communal homes run by charities. Another common example is the practice by community hospitals to receive poor, chronically ill patients from the government hospitals in return for approval to raise funds from the public to cover the shortfalls in their expenditures. On average, the government pays half the expenses and the patients pay about 10% and the balance is paid for by the general public via donations to the charities.

The citizen-government partnership in social equity works rather well. Although home ownership in Singapore is above 95%, there has not been any subprime crisis. The Singapore dollar did not fall when Singapore experienced a negative 16.4% fall in GDP in the fourth quarter of 2008, which protected the purchasing power of savings. The average household has six dollars in assets for every dollar in liabilities. But the 2008 Global Financial Crisis was a severe one. How the citizen-government partnership copes with this crisis is discussed later in this chapter.

Helping Low Skilled Singaporeans Cope with Foreign Workers

There is no minimum wage in Singapore. About 400,000 low-skilled Singaporeans have to compete directly with more than 500,000 low-skilled foreign workers. Since the individual responsibility approach requires Singaporeans to earn their living during their active years, the employment prospects and earnings of low-skilled Singaporeans must be protected from the influx of foreign workers because foreign workers have much lower reservation wages. As a result, employers of foreign workers are required to pay a monthly foreign worker levy of S$300 to S$450 per foreign worker. Although Singapore does not have unemployment benefits, we have a Workfare Scheme according to which any Singaporean worker earning less than S$1,500 monthly is provided a wage subsidy. For instance, a person earning S$800 a month can expect to receive S$100 a month, of which S$71 is channeled into his CPF account. In January 2008, 287,000 Singaporean workers received a total of S$146 million in wage subsidies from the government.

Saving Jobs During the Global Financial Crisis

As a small open economy where trade is more than three times GDP, the Singapore economy is very vulnerable to the global financial crisis. Under such conditions, the individual responsibility role will be in jeopardy. If people lose their jobs and therefore cannot save for old age, the government will have to foot ever-increasing bills for social security down the road. Hence, in the Singapore Budget for 2009, the government designed a jobs credit scheme under which employers receive a 12% cash grant on the first S$2,500 of each month's wages for each employee on their CPF payroll for one year in the first instance. This means that employers employing Singaporeans and permanent residents will find that their employers' CPF contribution rate is reduced by 9%.

In addition to the Jobs Credit Scheme, Budget FY2009 also introduced the Skills Programme for Up-grading and Resilience (SPUR). SPUR will pay 90% of the cost of training and 90% of absentee payrolls for workers who take part in the programme. This means that firms in will pay only 10% of their workers' wages if they send their workers for training. All these schemes prevented firms from retrenching workers. Singapore's GDP fell by 10% in the last quarter of 2008 compared to the first quarter of 2009, but the unemployment rate rose only from 2.5% to 3.1% over the same period.[120]

---

[120] According to the National Wages Council, Singapore's wage fixing institution, 66% of 1,900 firms surveyed in March 2009 stated that they would not retrench workers. About 1,400 companies have committed themselves to sending a total of 94,000 workers for training to take advantage of SPUR.

The costs of the Jobs Credit System and SPUR are funded by past reserves of about S\$7 billion. Budget FY2009 also provided economic assistance to low-income Singaporeans families via various schemes such as the Sales Tax Credit, costing the government S\$580 million. During the crisis in 2008 and 2009, some citizens were forced to sell their HDB flats or private flats and therefore suffered a severe capital loss. Some of them could not afford to buy another HDB flat. Consequently, the demand for one room rental HDB flats is now in short supply. The HDB has speeded up the construction of rental flats and increased the construction of four- and five-room flats in order to moderate prices in the re-sales market.

The Citizen-government partnership has entered into a new era. In the past when there was a crisis, the employer's CPF contribution rate would be reduced to protect employment and workers suffered a reduction in CPF savings. But in 2009, the government decided to use past reserves to protect jobs through the Jobs Credit Scheme and SPUR. Hence, the citizen-government partnership has strengthened and the government has kept its promise to protect both jobs and the purchasing power of savings.

Each year, the government shares the budget surplus with its citizens but most of these extras do not help the poor in a sustained manner. We are of the view that budget surpluses can be better spent if they are used to subsidize life insurance premiums and healthcare insurance for low income citizens, which should be made compulsory. Poor citizens who cannot not afford the premiums on a regular basis can then be helped through the citizen-partnership model.

CHALLENGES

GDP fell in 2009 by 2.1% but the Singapore economy is now expected to grow between 13% and 15% in 2010. The unemployment rate is around 2.3% and in 2010 we may import 100,000 foreigners into our workforce. Although, as in many Asian cities, Singapore has experienced asset inflation, first time buyers can still afford HDB flats.

Singapore's citizen-government partnership of ensuring social equity has been achieved and dignity preserved, with the elderly assured of a stream of income for as long as they live without being a heavy burden on the government. Singapore's model is sustainable provided the quality of her government remains high, there is a strong incentive to work, there is investment in training so that the workforce is employable, mandatory individual savings can be converted into an individual annuity scheme for most citizens, housing, healthcare and education remain affordable with the aid of state subsidies, prudent measures are used to look after the poor without creating disincentives to work and the individual responsibility approach is safeguarded in the event of economic crises.

The benefits of a successful citizen-government partnership in the provision of social equity are, therefore, adequate GDP growth, low inflation, low unemployment, a stable currency, affordable basic necessities such as housing, healthcare and education and sizable foreign reserves for emergencies.

END NOTES

Chan, A (2001). *Singapore's Changing Age Structure and the Policy Implications for Financial Security, Employment, Living Arrangements and Health Care.* Asia Meta Centre for Population and Sustainable Development Analysis, National University of Singapore, Singapore.

Chan, R and K A Wong (1998). The adequacy of the CPF account for retirement benefits in Singapore. *Singapore International Insurance and Actuarial Journal,* 19(2), 1–16.

Chew, R and S B Chew (2003). Employment relations in Singapore: From flexible wage system to flexible employment system? *Employment Relations Record (Australia),* 3(1), 53–63.

Chew, R and S B Chew (2005). Wage issues and human resources in Singapore. *Journal of Comparative Asian Development (United States),* 4(1), 77–103.

Chew, S B and R Chew (2008). Macro objectives of the central provident fund: A review. In Chia Wai Mun and Sng Hui Ying (eds.), *Singapore and Asia in a Globalised World.* Singapore: World Scientific.

Chia, N C and A Tsui (2003). Life annuities of compulsory savings and income adequacy of the elderly in Singapore. *Journal of Pension Economics and Finance*, 2(1), 41–65.

Feldstein, M (1996). The missing piece in policy analysis and social security reform. *The American Economic Review*, 86(2), 1–14.

Gillion, C, J Turner, C Bailey and D Latulippe D (2000). *Social Security Pensions; Development and Reform*. Geneva: International Labour Organisation.

Lim, C Y and Associates (1988). *Policy Options for the Singapore Economy*. Singapore: McGraw Hill.

Lim, C Y (2009). *Southeast Asia: The Long Road Ahead*. Singapore: World Scientific.

Reisman, D (2007). Housing and superannuation: Social security in Singapore. *International Journal of Social Economics*, 34(3), 159.

INDEX